A JOURNEY OF RICHES

DISCOVERING LOVE AND GRATITUDE

10 Stories that will open your mind and heart

A Journey Of Riches- Discovering Love and Gratitude

10 Stories that will open your mind and heart © 2018

Spender, John

Copyright © 2018 John Spender

This work is copyright. Apart from any use as permitted under the Copyright Act 1968, no part may be reproduced, copied, scanned, stored in a retrieval system, recorded or transmitted, in any form or by any means, without the prior permission of the publisher.

The rights of John Spender to be identified as the primary author of this work has been asserted by him under the Copyright Amendment (Moral Rights) Act 2000 Disclaimer.

The author and publishers have used their best efforts in preparing this book and disclaim liability arising directly and indirectly, consequential or otherwise from its contents.

All reasonable efforts have been made to obtain necessary copyright permissions. Any omissions or errors are unintentional and will, if brought to the attention of the publishers, be corrected in future impressions and printings.

Published by Motion Media International

Editing:Gwendolyn Parker, Nicole Policarpio, Chris Drabenstott.

Cover Design: Motion Media International

Typesetting & Assembly: Motion Media International

Printing: Create Space

Creator: Spender, John - Primary Author

Title: *A Journey Of Riches- Discovering Love and Gratitude*

10 Stories that will open your mind and heart

ISBN Print: 978-0-6482845-7-4

ISBN Digital: 978-0-6482845-8-1

Subjects: Self-Help, Motivation/Inspiration and Spirituality.

Acknowledgments

Reading and writing is a gift that too few gift to themselves. It is such a powerful way to reflect and gain closure from the past, reading and writing is a therapeutic process. The experience raises one's self-esteem, confidence, and awareness of self.

I learned this when I created the first book in the *A Journey Of Riches* series, which is, now one of thirteen books with over 140 different co-authors from thirty-three different countries. It's not easy to write about your own personal experience's and I honor and respect every one of the authors who has collaborated in the series thus far. For many of the authors, English is their second language, which is a significant achievement within its self.

In curating this anthology of short stories, I have been touched by the amount of generosity, gratitude, and shared energy that this experience has given everyone.

The idea for this book came from Wendy Jarvis the author of book 11 *Finding Inspiration* while we were editing her chapter. Initially, Wendy was going to write in book nine *Transformation Calling* but was unable to make the due date, because of some personal reasons. When the editor and I read Wendy's chapter, it was all about love and gratitude and not really about inspiration, and so the idea was born for book 13 in the series. We hope that this book will open your mind, heart to embrace and be open to the world at large. Here it is book 13 in the *A Journey Of Riches* series *Discovering Love and Gratitude*, 10 Stories that will open your mind and heart. Of course, I could not have created this book without the nine other co-authors who each said YES when I asked them to share their insights into how they found and find love and gratitude in their life. Just like each chapter in this book makes for inspiring reading, each story represents one chapter in the presence of each of the authors, with the chief aim of having you, the reader, living a more loving and appreciative life.

I'd like to thank all the authors for entrusting me with their unique memories, encounters, and wisdom. Thank you for sharing and opening the door to your soul so that others may learn from your experience, may the readers glean confidence from your successes and wisdom from your failures.

Thank you to my family, I know you are proud of me and how far I have come from that 10-year-old boy who was learning how to read and write at a fundamental level. Mom, Robert, Dad, Merril, my brother Adam and his daughter Krystal, my sister Hollie, her partner Brian, my nephew Charlie and my niece, Heidi. Also my grandparents Gran and Pop who are alive and well and Ma and Pa who now rest in peace. They accept me just the way I am with all my travels and adventures around the world.

Thanks to all the team at MotionMediaInternational who have done an excellent job at editing and collating this book. It has been a pleasure working with you all on this successful project, and I thank you for your patience in dealing with the various changes and adjustments along the way.

Thank you, the reader for having the courage to look at your life and how you can improve your future in a fast and rapidly changing world.

And I'd enjoy connecting with readers, as I love sharing stories.

You can email me here: jrspender7@gmail.com

Acknowledgments

Thank you again to my fellow co-authors: Marina Pearson, Gretchen Phillips-Williams, Cheryl Maria Marella, Leanne Cordova, Tasha Dietha Amanda, Fernanda Lorenti, Manale Akkad, Pendek Sitong, Eui J Jung.

I hope you have enjoyed, this co-authored experience as much as I have. Love and light.

With gratitude

John Spender

Praise for A Journey Of Riches book series.

"If you are looking for an inspiring read to get you through any change, this is it!! This book is filled with many gripping perspectives, from a collection of successful international authors with a tonne of wisdom to share."

~ Theera Phetmalaigul, Entrepreneur/Investor.

"*A Journey Of Riches* is an empowering series that implements two simple words in overcoming life's struggles.

By diving into the meaning of the words "problem" and "challenge," you will find yourself motivated to believe in the triumph of perseverance. With many different authors from all around the world, coming together to share different stories of life's trials, you will find yourself drenched in encouragement to push through even the darkest of battles.

The stories are heartfelt personal shares of moving through and transforming challenges into rich life experiences.

The book will move, touch and inspire your spirit to face and overcome any of life's adversities. A truly inspirational read. Thank you for being the kind open soul you are John!!"

~ Casey Plouffe, Seven Figure Network Marketer.

"A must-read for anyone facing major changes or challenges in life right now. This book will give you the courage to move through any challenge with confidence, grace, and ease."

~ Jo-Anne Irwin - Transformational Coach & Best Selling Author.

"I'm a fan of self-help books, and I read them a lot. I love this book and the stories that are contained within them, but most of all I like the concept. I love that John Spender decided to do an anthology of stories from inspirational people. This book is the type of book where you can either choose to be inspired by ten different stories or choose a chapter that resonates with you the most.

As I read this book, it confirmed to me my life suspicion that things happen beyond our control. It can be incredibly devastating at times. It is those moments that bring us to our knees not knowing whether we can or even want to stand anymore. But, in these challenging moments, this book confirms to me that we do have one choice we can let go, make changes and embrace the new. It's the choice of how we decide to view these hardships. Our perspective determines what our life will be after these moments in our lives.

Some very heart-wrenching stories were contained in these books. Some of them I even had to ask myself, "How do you even recover from a situation like that?"

Perspective. It all boils down to how we decide to view those hard challenges that come our way. At least that is what I took away from this book.

Thank you to John and his team of authors for getting together to create this book."

~ Kit Zakimi on Amazon.

"I have enjoyed the *Journey of Riches* book series. Each person's story is written from the heart and everyone's journey different. We all have a story to tell, and John Spender does an amazing job of finding authors and combining their stories, into uplifting books."

Praise for a Journey of Riches book series.

~ Liz Misner Palmer, Foreign Service Officer.

"A timely read as I'm facing a few changes right now. I liked the various insights from the different authors. This book will inspire you to move through any challenge or change that you are experiencing."

~ David Ostrand, Business Owner.

"I've known John Spender for a while now, and I was blessed with an opportunity to be in book four in the series. I know that you will enjoy this new journey like the rest of the books in the series. The collection of stories will assist you with making changes, to deal with challenges and to see that transformation is possible for your life."

~Charlie O'shea, Entrepreneur.

"A Journey of Riches series will draw you in and help you dig deep into your soul. Every author has an unbelievable life story of purpose inside of them. John Spender is dedicated to bringing peace, love, and adventure to the world of his readers! Dive into this series, and you will be transformed!!"

~ Jeana Matichak, Author of Finding Peace.

"Awesome! Truly inspirational! It is amazing what the human spirit can achieve and overcome! Highly recommended!!"

~Fabrice Beliard, Australian Business Coach, and Best Selling Author.

"*A Journey of Riches* Series is a must read. It is an empowering collection of inspirational and moving stories full of courage, strength, and heart. Bringing peace and awareness to those lucky enough to read to assist and inspire them on their life journey."

Gemma Castiglia, Avalon Healing, Best Selling Author.

"The *A Journey of Riches* book series is an inspirational collection of books that will empower you to take on any challenge or change in life."

~Kay Newton, Midlife Stress Buster, and Best Selling Author.

"*A Journey of Riches* book series is an inspiring collection of stories, sharing many different ideas and perspectives on how to overcome challenges, deal with change and to make empowering choices in your life. Open the book anywhere and let your mood chose where you need to read. Buy one of the books today; you'll be glad that you did! "

~Trish Rock, Modern Day Intuitive, Bestselling Author, Speaker, Psychic & Holistic Coach.

"Transformational Change is another inspiring read in the *A Journey of Riches* book series. The authors are from all over the world, and each has a unique perspective to share, that will have you thinking differently about your current circumstances in life. An inspiring read!"

~Alexandria Calamel, Success Coach and Best Selling Author.

"The A Journey of Riches books is a collection of real-life stories, which are truly inspiring and give you the confidence that no matter what you are dealing with in your life, that there is a light at the end of the tunnel, and a very bright one at that.

Totally empowering!"

~ John Abbott, Freedom Entrepreneur.

"An amazing collection of true stories from individuals who have overcome great changes and who have transformed their lives and used their experience to uplift, inspire and support others."

~Carol Williams, Author-Speaker-Coach.

"You can empower yourself from the power within this book, that can help awaken the sleeping giant within you. John has a purpose in life

Praise for A Journey of Riches Book Series.

to bring inspiring people together to share their wisdom, for the benefit of all who venture deep into this book Transformational Change. If you are looking for inspiration to be someone special in this book can be your guide."

~Bill Bilwani, Renown Melbourne Restaurateur.

"In the A Journey Of Riches series, you will catch the impulse to step up, reconsider and settle for only the very best for yourself and those around you. Penned from the heart and with an unflinching drive to make a difference for the good of all, *A Journey Of Riches* series is a must-read."

~Steve Coleman Author of "Decisions, Decisions! How to Make the Right One Every Time."

"If you want to be on top of your game? *A Journey of Riches* is a must read with breakthrough insights that will help you do just that!"

~ Christopher Chen, Entrepreneur.

"In *A Journey of Riches*, you will find the insight, resources, and tools you need to transform your life. By reading the authors stories, you too can be inspired to achieve your greatest accomplishments and what is truly possible for you. Reading this book activates your true potential for transforming, you're life way beyond what you think is possible. Read it and learn how you too can have a magical life."

~Elaine Mc Guinness, Bestselling Author of Unleash Your Authentic Self!

"If you are looking for an inspiring read look no further than the *A Journey Of Riches* book series. The books are an inspiring collection of short stories, that will encourage you to embrace life even more. I highly recommend you read one of the books today!"

~Kara Dono, Doula, Healer and Best Selling Author.

"*A Journey of Riches* series is a must-read for anyone seeking to enrich their own lives and gain wisdom through the wonderful stories of personal empowerment & triumphs over life's challenges. I've given several copies to my family, friends, and clients to inspire and support them to step into their greatness. I highly recommend that you read these books, savoring the many aha's and tools you will discover inside."

~Michele Cempaka, Hypnotherapist, Shaman, Transformational Coach & Reiki Master.

"If you are looking for an inspirational read, look no further than the *A Journey Of Riches* book series. The books are an inspiring and educational collection of short stories from the author's soul itself, that will encourage you to embrace life even more. I've even given them to my clients too so that they are inspired by their journeys in life, wealth, health and everything else in between.

I recommend you make it a priority, to read one of the books today!"

~Goro Gupta, Chief Education Officer, Mortgage Terminator, Property Mentor.

"The *A Journey Of Riches* book series is filled with real-life short stories of heartfelt tribulations turned into uplifting, self-transformation by the power of the human spirit to overcome adversity. The journeys captured in these books will encourage you to embrace life in a whole new way.

I highly recommend reading this inspiring anthology series."

~Chris Drabenstott, Best Selling Author, and Editor.

"There is so much motivational power in the *A Journey of Riches* series!! Each book is a compilation of inspiring, real-life stories by several different authors, which makes the journey feel more relatable

PRAISE FOR A JOURNEY OF RICHES BOOK SERIES.

and success more attainable. If you are looking for something to move you forward, you'll find it in one (or all) of these books."

~Cary Mac Arthur, Personal Empowerment Coach

"I've been fortunate to write with John Spender and now call him a friend. *A Journey of Riches* book series features real stories that have inspired me and will inspire you. John has a passion for finding amazing people from all over the world, giving the series a global perspective on relevant subject matters."

~Mike Campbell, Fat Guy Diary, LLC

"The *A Journey of Riches* series, is the reflection of beautiful souls who have discovered the fire within. Each story takes you inside the truth of what truly matters in life. While reading these stories, my heart space expanded to understand that our most significant contribution in this lifetime is to give and receive love. May you also feel inspired as you read this book." ~Katie Neubaum, Author of Transformation Calling.

TABLE OF CONTENTS

Introduction 1
Chapter One: Farm Life - Lessen's For Life *(John Spender)* 5
Chapter Two: This Is Me: From Frazzled To Free *(Marina Pearson)* 15
Chapter Three: Life-Long Learning Journey *(Gretchen Phillips-Williams)* 25
Chapter Four: Love And Gratitude, The Antidote
       To My Darkness *(Cheryl Maria Marella)* 37
Chapter Five: Life-Building Dreams *(Leanne Cordova)* 49
Chapter Six: The Joy of Motherhood *(Fernanda Lorenti)* 61
Chapter Seven: Small Wins *(Manal Akkad)* 71
Chapter Eight: A Little Story From QZ8501 *(Tasha Dietha Amanda)* 87
Chapter Nine: Love from Within *(Pendek Sitong)* 101
Chapter Ten: Over and Beyond *(Trauma Eui J Jung)* 115
Author Biographies 127
    John Spender 127
    Marina Pearson 129
    Gretchen Phillips-Williams 130
    Cheryl Maria Marella 132
    Leanne Cordova 133
    Fernanda Lorenti 135
    Manal Akkad 136
    Tasha Dietha Amanda 138
    Pendek Sitong 139
    Eui J Jung 141
Afterword 143

Introduction

I created this book and chose the different authors to share their insights, wisdom, and experiences to assist people who may be going through challenges, adversities, or changes similar to those of the authors.

Like all of us, each author has a unique story and insight to share with you. It just may be the case, that one or more of these authors have lived through an experience that is similar to circumstances in your life right now. Their words could be just the words you need to read to help you through your challenges. Perhaps reading about one or more of these experiences will fill in the missing piece of your puzzle, so to speak, allowing you to move forward into the next phase of your journey.

Storytelling has been the way humankind has communicated ideas and learning throughout our civilization. While we have become more sophisticated with technology, and life in the modern world is more convenient, there is still much discontent and dissatisfaction with one's reality. Many people have also moved away from reading books, and they are missing out on valuable information that can help them to move forward in life, with a positive outlook. I think it is essential to turn off the T.V., to slow down, and to read, reflect, and take the time to appreciate everything you have in life.

I like anthology books because they carry many different perspectives and insights on a singular topic. I find that sometimes when I'm reading a book that has just one author I gain an understanding of their viewpoint and writing style very quickly and the reading becomes predictable. With this book and all of the books in the *A Journey of Riches* book series, you have many different writing styles and viewpoints that will help shape your perspective towards your current set of circumstances.

Anthology books are also great because you can start from any chapter and gain a valuable insight or a nugget of wisdom without the feeling that you have missed something from the earlier chapters.

I love reading many different types of personal development books because learning and personal growth are vital to me. If you are not learning and growing, well, you're staying the same. Everything in the universe is growing, expanding, and changing. If we are not open to different ideas and different ways of thinking and being, then we can become close-minded.

The concept of this book series is to open you up to different ways of perceiving your reality, to give you hope, to encourage you, and to give you many avenues of thinking about the same subject. My wish for you is to feel empowered to make a decision that will best suit you in moving forward with your life. As Albert Einstein said, **"We cannot solve problems with the same level of thinking that created them."**

Introduction

With Einstein's words in mind, let your mood pick a chapter in the book or read from the beginning to the end and allow yourself to be guided to find the answers you seek.

With gratitude

John Spender

"Gratitude is the open door to the power, the wisdom and the creativity of the universe. You open the door through Gratitude."

~ Deepak Chopra

CHAPTER ONE

Farm Life - Lessen's For Life

By John Spender

The stars shone so brightly in the sky as if appearing for the first time. The sounds of the night were echoing through the warm spring evening. The crickets were especially loud. My pop said that meant it was going to be a hot summer. You could hear the frogs croaking in unison. The entire bushland was alive with sound, which was music to my ears filling me with a tickle of joy. From our spot on the hill just behind my grandparents' quaint farmhouse, my mom and I sat in appreciation of the glorious night sky not uttering a word. The last few months had been incredibly difficult on my mother and I knew she needed my presence more than ever, or at least as much as a six-year-old could offer. As we snuggled together, a shooting star blazed across the sky. We gasped with excitement, and I knew we had witnessed something special. My mom kissed me on my forehead. It was a kiss filled with love and pride and one of relief as if the shooting star had been a sign that everything was going to be okay. No matter what happened in my life, at a deep level, I knew my mother loved me so much more than words could ever describe. We were going to be okay, and this move to the farm had been for her kids.

Gratitude is the memory of the heart ~ Jean Baptiste Massieu

Only a couple of months earlier it was a delightful surprise to see my Uncle Peter with my canteen lunch, a meat pie with tomato sauce, one of my favorite lunches at the time. He said, "We are going on an adventure, and your mom will be waiting for us." Manly, in the northern beaches of Sydney, is at the end of a peninsula overlooking the open ocean on one side and converging with bushland on the other side overlooking Sydney Harbor. This was home for the next six weeks until mom could get enough money together for the nine-hour train ride to my pop and gran's farm in northern New South Wales. My mom was working, so Adam and I did whatever we wanted during the day. We didn't have much money as a family and none ourselves. We often visited the local video arcade and watched the other kids playing the machines. The beaches in this area are amazing. We would swim, build sand castles, and even collect blue bottles (jellyfish). It was also the very first time that I ever shopped lifted. We mostly stole lollies, chocolate, and even a big candy lollipop.

Dad came to visit us, and he expressed how sorry he was, but you could tell by the mood that we weren't going back. It had become unsafe in our family home, and my dad seemed disinterested in raising a loving family. The turning point was when my dad took a two-week leave from the Navy to watch the 1982 Brisbane Commonwealth Games on T.V. That was the straw that broke the camel's back for my mother, as she later told me. Back in those days, my dad's main priorities were providing for his family, swimming, watching the news, and—his all-time favorite—sports! Dad had a hard time dealing with his emotions and was ruled by his upbringing. His now-wife told me that one year when he was 10, my ma said he had been naughty just before Christmas, and he never received any presents. That must have been incredibly difficult to take, but at some point, one has to take responsibly for the decisions they make. Both me and my older brother, Adam, copped strappings over small, petty things. One time, I had placed shells in our newly concreted driveway. My cousin, Paul, had told on me, and I received the dreaded bare-bum strapping. My mom later revealed to me that Adam got the buckle end of the strap as a five-year-old resulting in a nasty wound to his bottom, unable to sit on a chair for a couple of weeks. Naturally, the school wanted to talk to my parents. Mom said dad refused to attend their request for a meeting, so my mom went alone.

I remember when my dad had been away for a few weeks at sea with the Navy, where he was the chief petty officer. On his return, we were all very excited to see him, and we ran to the door as we heard his car pull into the driveway. We could see him through the front window as Mom had put the front light on earlier. With us three kids standing behind the door, Adam put the lock chain on right when my dad was opening the door, and the door only opened an inch, keeping my dad outside. He was furious and with a shout demanded that the door is opened immediately. I panicked and were almost as tall as my brother I reached up and removed the keychain lock from the latch. Yelling with fury, my dad entered the house and blamed me for locking him out for all but five seconds. No one else dared to say a word, especially Adam after his last hiding. My father took me into his room before I spoke a word, pulled down my PJ bottoms, and gave me a flogging that I'll never forget, both from the pain I felt as well as the injustice of the situation. I was only five, and I hadn't done anything wrong. It wasn't long after this incident that my dad returned home to an empty house. He later told me that all my mother had left a knife and fork, a plate, a bowl, and a spoon. Talk about a wake-up call! My dad had a strong work ethic. He believed in doing the right thing for the sake of doing the right thing, but he didn't always get that right. He rarely drank, he never smoked, and he was totally against drugs. Although my dad was a strict disciplinarian, his way of showing his love was through providing for his family. His dominate controlling nature came as a result of him not feeling worthy or empowered as a man, along with his inability to express how he was feeling emotionally.

"People who love themselves, don't hurt other people. The more we hate ourselves, the more we want others to suffer."
~ Dan Pearce

I resented him for many years, for his strict disciplinarian nature, with wanting things to be a certain way and getting angry over petty things that were irrelevant to the bigger picture of living a happy life. You can discover the strangest things about yourself when you take an honest look at how you are showing up in life, especially when you get curious as to why you do what you do. After spending a weekend at a Mitchell J. Behan (MJB) personal development seminar in Melbourne, I recognized that the very behaviors I resented in my father were evident in how I was acting out in my business with my employees. I expected them to be on time, I had a strict sense of discipline about the way I ran my business, and I would often get upset with them over the pettiest of things. I realized that the very behaviors I was resenting in my father were the same behaviors I was demonstrating in my own life. At this moment, I realized that there wasn't really anything to forgive and simultaneously I was overcome with an overwhelming sensation of love and gratitude emanating from my body. I came to appreciate my dad and what he went through in his own life. It dawned on me that, in the bigger scheme of our reality, every experience has equal amounts of negatives and positives, and when we deem an experience, negatively we are negating the positives of that peculiar experience and vice versa.

My father being heavy handed when I was a child taught me to be strong both mentally and physically, as well as caused me to adopt a dogged sense of determination and a strong will. I benefited from that experience just as much as I had suffered. When you see this, the experience is automatically calibrated. The lopsided emotional hold dissipates like steam flying out of a kettle on full boil. You become centered in the core of your being; it's a freeing and liberating experience. I now have a decent relationship with my dad, and we celebrated his 70th birthday recently in Adelaide where he now lives. I'm grateful for the role he has played in my life.

"Gratitude turns everything into a gift." ~Anonymous

My pop was the father figure to us three kids in those early years. He would get us up early to milk the cow into a bucket, milk that would be for our cereal. We collected the chicken eggs, picked oranges and lemons for our juices, fruits which were growing from the same tree after my pop had grafted them together. This was the ritual we followed each morning before we went to school. We would walk three kilometers down a dirt road to the bus stop for a 30-minute trip to school. Adam was in grade three, I was in grade one, and our sister, Hollie, was in kindergarten. After school, we all wanted to help Pop with the chores on the farm. We would let the chooks out and feed the various animals. On the weekends, we would tidy up various paddocks, picking up sticks, branches and logs. We would play games to see who could pull out the most fire weeds, which left unchecked could spread like wildfire throughout the paddocks. Pop even had a system that taught us the value of fair exchange where, depending on how many chores we did, we would receive sweets. If we did something wrong, we would have lollies deducted. Pop treated us all the same. Hollie was so young that she would try to get out of doing her chores or just forget, and one particular week she received no lollies, which Adam and I thought was hilarious.

My grandma would prepare dinner every night, but before dinner, we would have to be showered and in our pj's. There wasn't a lot of water for our showers in those days on the farm, so Pop taught us how to have a quick shower which was pretty easy because the water was cold. You simply went underneath the shower to get wet then you turned the water off, soaped yourself all over and then you showered the soap off and you were done. Every night without fail we would get dessert, and my gran was the best at making desserts. She would make rice pudding or banana and ice cream or lemon meringue pie, fruit salad and ice cream, rhubarb with custard, and my personal favorite was mulberry pie with whipped cream and ice cream. We would pick the mulberries from the tree and even climb to the top to get the berries, eating some before we put most of them in our plastic bag. At times, Gran even made her own ice cream, which was delicious. Our gran wasn't the best at cooking meals because she used to stress out and always overcook the meat. We would never dare to complain, though, from fear of not getting any dessert.

Now and then, Pop would tell us stories of his life as a boxer, a young man growing up in Bondi, or when he used to collect for the various bookmakers in the eastern suburbs of Sydney. The one that really stuck in my head was when he was working as a stockman on the cattle stations, riding horseback in remote areas. I'll never forget the story of him riding through the desert and up ahead he could see a cluster of small trees and what looked like a man sitting underneath one of the trees wearing a broad-brimmed hat. As he rode closer, he nodded his head and received no response. All he could see was the whites of the man's eyes following him as he rode past. When he came much closer, he could clearly see that he wasn't looking at the whites of the man's eyes, but maggots! The poor bugger had run out of water and died. Pop had hundreds and hundreds of stories and yarns he would often tell us, mostly at the dinner table.

Our rooms were not far from the farmhouse. Pop converted an old shed into three rooms for us kids. At bedtime, Mom would walk us down. We would have torches, and quite often you could hear fruit bats landing in the abundance of fruit trees: mango trees, peaches, apricots, custard apples, lychees, and, of course, mulberry trees. Pop also had a decent-sized veggie patch, and most nights we had fresh vegetables from the garden. When helping Pop on the farm, he would give us lessons, and he had a favorite saying: "Keep your eyes and ears open and your mouth shut." He would say that all the time. This taught me to connect in with my surroundings and become observant. I loved the animals on the farm. Pop made his livelihood mostly from raising and selling sheep and Murray Grey cattle, and my gran always prepared all the meals. I would often observe the livestock, noticing how they interacted with each other, each having its own personality. It wasn't uncommon for me to be able to sit with the dairy cows and their calves as if I were one of their own. I remember watching a flock of sheep one day in a valley where the grass was always green because it was at the bottom of a large sloping embankment and received spillover from a big dam at the far end. I was watching the sheep from halfway down the embankment when I noticed one of the lambs was walking with a limp. It turns out that the lamb had a cyst in its leg, and my pop had to cut it out. These are some of the various memories flooding my mind as I share these experiences with you in appreciation for my pop.

'We often take for granted the very things that most deserve our gratitude.' ~ Cynthia Ozick

One of the lessons he consistently taught enhanced my memory by getting me to remember numbers. Other times it would be a certain word. At the end of whatever we were doing, but more often than not at the end of the day, he would ask me to recall the word or number. I enjoyed being able to remember the detail nine times out of ten. It wasn't until later in life that I realized he was training my memory recall, and this skill has served me well to this day. Often our sense of gratitude for childhood lessons and experiences comes much later in life, but it's a deeper sense of appreciation that lasts forever like a natural spring bubbling up from the core of who we are because of these very experiences.

Pop wasn't the type of person you wanted to disappoint, not because you would get into trouble or because he would say something; it was more to the point that he wouldn't say anything but expected a better standard from you. He wasn't a very tall man, certainly not an imposing figure. He was thoughtful, well-read, a good teacher, patient but would not put up with any non-sense, and he was disciplined and led by example. Farm life for my pop meant work. He had a strong work ethic, and he had a consistent daily routine: up early before breakfast, back to work for a couple of hours before smoko (morning tea), another couple of hours of work before lunch, and another two hours of work until afternoon tea, and again another couple of hours until dinner. This was daily except at muster times when he would leave early to track down all the cattle for drenching (worming), branding of the calves, and to castrate the young males. At one point, Pop had some 2,000 acres of land. Locating the cattle could be a little challenging, and then you had to round them up and herd them back to the stockyards. I was a little young for these trips, but my brother would go, and Pop would take his two kelpies, Dusty and Sally. They were well-trained and followed my pop's command. Dusty was a tan, brown color, and, although eager to please, he could be a little rough with the sheep especially, at times biting them. Sally was black, and her temperament was well-rounded, and she was skilled at mustering, never really getting too carried away with the excitement of it all.

When Pop and Adam brought the cattle back and rounded them up in the stockyard, I was allowed to help with the rest of the maintenance of the cattle. Pop had one prized bull, Ozzie, and he was a beast with a huge body, muscly shoulders, a broad head, and gigantic testicles the size of a football. I used to marvel at how big they were compared to my own. With balls like that, you can imagine that he was a top breeder, and he knew exactly when the heifers (female cows) were on heat, quite often several at one time, and he could effortlessly service all of them. I found it fascinating to watch Ozzie do this in less than 20 minutes.

Ozzie was getting a little long in the tooth, and Pop was wanting to introduce a younger bull, Ozzie 2, to the herd, but he was still young and not ready to be with so many heifers. He was in another paddock waiting until he came of age. The paddock was next to the stockyard, and Ozzie 2 was sniffing around the holding pen, which was next to his paddock. The problem was, Ozzie escaped from the stockyard with two heifers, and the two bulls started to wrestle with their heads. Ozzie was getting the better of the exchange, and it wasn't looking good for Ozzie 2. Adam and I alerted Pop, and he sprinted over to separate them. He was running over, and he ran straight into a temporary wire fence. Luckily, it didn't have any barbs, because he hit the fence at full speed, tumbled over, got straight back on his feet, and scared young Ozzie away before they killed each other. We were left standing in awe at Pop's commitment to avert a dangerous situation. These bulls cost a fortune, and he can't afford to let one of them get hurt, especially the younger bull. We both learned never to put two bulls near each other and Pop's mistake showed us that he was human after all.

There was never a dull moment on the farm, from having cow dung fights with my brother, to catching yabbies, to killing roosters for our Sunday roast, and the many day trips to national parks and the surrounding beaches…it was such a wholesome time in all our lives, and it was a gift that I'll cherish forever. Farm lessons are life lessons. Had my life stayed on its original course, I would have missed out on the wholeness and an earthy connection that farming gives you.

The circumstances that led us to grow up on the farm weren't fun to experience at the time and caused much confusion. I've learned that everything is divinely connected, and nothing is ever really missing in our lives. It may have appeared that I lost my dad at this time, but he appeared in the form of my pop, and this role has been taken on by many other people over the years, especially when my mother remarried. Dad came to visit once and took us up to see our ma and pa in Queensland, and we went to Sea World and Dream World. It was a real treat being able to go on so many amazing rides and watching the various shows. My dad tried the best he could to play a part in our lives. But the real grounding influence at this time came from Pop and his tough-love approach to life. I've learned that love and gratitude can be found in the strangest, most unlikely of places. Life and our environment are all designed to propel humanity forward, to help us expand and grow into better versions of ourselves. Sometimes that comes in the form of challenges and other times the form is more supportive in nature. Then we see that the balance of this love and gratitude becomes our natural state of being. Love and gratitude can be found in every life experience if we look at life in a certain kind of way.

"When we focus on our gratitude, the tide of disappointment goes out and the tide of love rushes in."

~ Kristin Armstrong

CHAPTER TWO

THIS IS ME: FROM FRAZZLED TO FREE

By Marina Pearson

What would happen if one day you discovered that who you thought you were was all made up? I remember when one of my friends asked me, "Who is the *I* that you refer to on a daily basis?" This stopped me in my tracks, as I had always assumed that the *I* I talked about was Marina—a woman, joy coach, *The Joy of Being* podcast host, divorcee, mum, investor—who is bilingual and lives in Javea, Spain. And while all of that is true, these are just labels I have given myself. Over time, I have come to see that I don't know who I am, as it changes moment to moment based on my thinking.

Yet, there is something that is constant—what some people call *essence*, *life force*, *spirit*, *soul*—but I will never truly discover what that is even though I have experienced it, as am sure you have, too. Words won't do it justice, but all I can say is that it's very quiet, and I am totally in the present moment and my mind is very quiet. Some call it *coming home*; I call it *sitting in your true being.* Nevertheless, if you are reading this and thinking, *I have never experienced that before,* then let me suggest that you have, but you may not remember it or would have named it as such. We all have the capacity for sitting in our true being and experiencing it, and this can be done through your innate capacity to have insights, which quieten the mind and give you access to the beautiful feeling that you are.

I know that, for me, the days of spending months in depression and upset have disappeared and, instead, my new normal looks like one of peace and tranquillity with the occasional glimpse of low moments. This translates into spending less time in the experience of not being enough versus knowing that I am enough regardless of what my life or circumstances look like. I have seen my perception of who I thought I was change time and time again, but there have been specific insights that have challenged the way I have seen things as truth.

My Father's Death

My father passed away with pneumonia at Basingstoke Hospital, UK, on the evening of January 17, 2012, at the age of ninety-two, and I was very lucky to be by his side when he did. We had become close during the last years of his life, but it hadn't always been that way.

My father was an eccentric type. He would show up at my school sometimes with his slippers and dressing gown on. And on one of those really lucky days, he came to school without his teeth in either! There was a big age gap between my mother and father, so when he turned up like this at school, I used to tell my friends he was my granddad because I was so embarrassed. Nothing like your dad turning up to school without false teeth and wearing slippers to really ruin your street cred at the age of eleven. I guess, as a little girl, I didn't understand how his upbringing had affected his capacity to be with a child and understand her. He had a harsh Victorian upbringing where children were seen and not heard, and the relationship with his dad had been a difficult one.

He was brought up by his nannies and barely saw his parents, and during the little time that he did see them, his encounters with his dad were always hard. And, so, bearing this in mind, it's not surprising that he didn't really know how to be around a small girl, which is why we didn't have much of a relationship until a long time later, until I was able to understand why he found it so difficult to relate to me.

However, in 2008 when my first marriage failed, I went back to live in London, and it was there that my relationship with him started to change. We started to spend more time together and I began to see his personal struggles as just that, nothing to do with me. Understanding his struggles with his parents made it easier for me to put aside my judgments of him and see him for the wonderfully talented and witty human being that he was.

When my sister phoned me that morning to tell me he had been rushed to hospital, my first thought was that he would be fine. It wasn't the first time I would be visiting him in hospital, as I had done so many times previously, and he had always bounced back, so I wasn't too worried.

However, when I entered his room, I experienced a very different picture from the one that I had imagined. To be honest, I was not ready for what I was about to experience.

I walked into a frenetic environment with nurses coming in and out every hour to ensure that my father was comfortable. However, it was quite clear to me that pneumonia had started to affect his cognition. He was finding it difficult to be coherent and would come in and out of recognizing me and was confused about what he actually wanted. One moment he wanted food, and the next moment he didn't. The next moment he wanted to leave, and then he wanted to stay and rest. From one moment to the next, he would recognize me, and then he couldn't.

This played out until about 7 p.m. It was at this point that everything went quiet. The nurses had stopped coming into the room. He was sitting on the chair while I was on the bed holding his hand as we watched the 7 o'clock news together. As I lay there, I suddenly felt his hand go weak in mine. As I noticed, I turned to him, and it looked like he had just fallen asleep. It was at this point that I realised he had taken his last breath. Despite the context, it was a beautiful moment that I will treasure forever.

As I processed what had happened, I ran out to get a nurse, and at that point my sister arrived. As my father was carried off to another room, I was given some time to decide whether I wanted to go in and see him. I resisted for a moment and then decided to visit with him one last time. And I am glad that I did, as it gave me a huge insight into who we are and what we are made of.

I walked into the room where he lay and, to my absolute surprise, he didn't look like my dad at all. His passing had taken 50 years off him. He looked translucent and at peace. All his frown lines and stress lines had gone. COMPLETELY gone. And it was at this point when I realized that who he was wasn't his body; if it had been, then he wouldn't have looked so different.

A few years later, it dawned on me as I was reflecting back on that moment: our body was given to us to be able to experience life. We need to inhabit this body for us to see, hear, smell, and touch. It's the container which we inhabit to get us around and to experience the pain and pleasures that are available to us. In fact, it became clear to me that without our bodies we are not able to even perceive. It's an incredible instrument created by the same intelligence who created all of us.

What Pregnancy Taught Me About Who We Are

The second insight I had about our true nature came out of the blue when I was walking down the streets of London and I was three months pregnant with my son, Leo. As I was walking down the street, a new thought popped in, which was, "What is growing Leo?" I knew I wasn't. After all I didn't have to think him into existence, and I didn't need to do anything actively, as a natural process was taking care of that. And then I got curious about what was creating him.

What was giving him a nose, an eye, a mouth, a liver? What was creating this incredible organism and being. And then it hit me. It's the same energy that created the sun, the mountains, the sea, and all that we experience in nature. The same universal energy and intelligence, which gives life to everything. Some like to call it god; others like to call it love or the universe. Whatever you call it, it is what you are. We are made of that. At one point, we were formless, and this energy brought us into the form so that we could experience our life here on earth.

It was here that tears started to run down my face, as I was in awe of this magic, of this truth, of the grand design that unifies us all. And in that moment I felt as one with everything around me. It was in this moment that I saw how we are all one. If we come from the same energy that births life, then there cannot be any separation—only the illusion of it. Everything that is created is done so by this energy, and there is no exception. Life is life-ing and we are a conduit for it. If that is the case, we cannot be our thoughts. It's the fact that we have the capacity to think that's important, not the content.

What Lying in a Bed in Bali Taught Me

For many years, I had bought into the notion of who I am as being a fixed thing. *I am Marina, who is this way.* I believed the bull crap I would say to myself about who I *thought* I was, and it didn't look pretty—especially during my teenage years. By the time I was thirteen or fourteen, I believed all the bad things I would say about myself. I am fat, ugly, stupid, unpopular...and so the list went on. So, as a result, in an effort to not see myself this way, I decided to stop eating and became anorexic. I believed that if I were beautiful and thin enough I would be lovable. Over time, these voices in my head became louder and louder, until one day I decided I had enough and headed out to buy some sleeping pills to end my life. I remember that day as if it only happened yesterday. And as I lay there waiting for the pills to kick in, the inner voice of me told me off and urged me to go down the stairs, tell someone what I had done, and then call an ambulance. And that's what happened.

I am so grateful for that day, as it marked the first step towards a path of healing, a path which has taken me from believing what I see of myself as totally true to seeing those voices in my head as just voices. In fact, during the first three months of my pregnancy, I spent a lot of time in bed because I was so tired. One night, as I was lying there alone, the question of *Who am I?* popped into my head. I didn't really know how to answer this. So, I didn't. And a few seconds later, I heard, "I AM." I waited a little longer to find out what I was, but there was silence after it. It then dawned on me that there was nothing to go after it. By putting something in front of I AM would mean that it was just another construct, just another belief that I had made up about myself. Because who I am has no name.

It's intangible.

I AM.

And that is the same for all of us. We are not what we label ourselves, not the roles or jobs we have. Those things are what we do, not what we are.

You Are Not Your Roles or Your Feelings

As I have already shared, we are capable of giving ourselves labels and roles, but they don't need to define us. But I haven't always seen it this way. I used to think that my identity had something to do with the roles I played, which meant that for every role I also had a story attached to it which I very much identified with.

It just so happens that I work with a lot of mothers in business who innocently mistake their different roles for who they are. So, they may wear many different hats, such as mum, business owner, wife, sibling, or divorcee. All of these roles have lots of meaning for them, as they do for everyone, including you. But it's so easy for all of us to fall into this trap from time to time. After all, when asked what you do, we usually reply with *I am_____,* as opposed to, *I do this or that.*

When I work with clients who are in their own identity traps, I show them this model, which opens their eyes to a new way of seeing themselves:

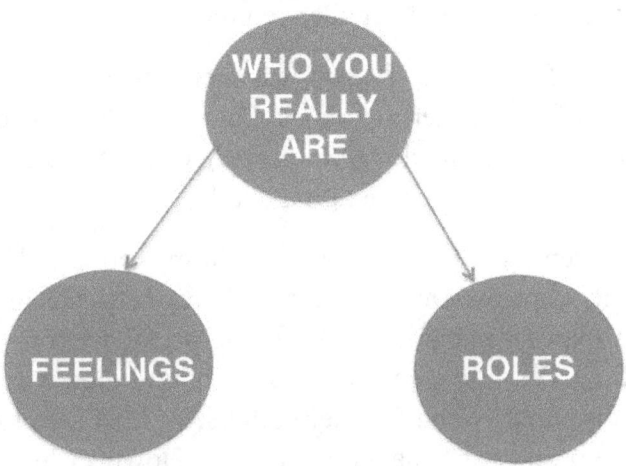

The basic premise of this little diagram is that you are not your feelings or your roles. Let's start with the feelings part. Have you ever said to yourself I AM TIRED, or I AM OVERWHELMED, or I AM SAD, or I AM DEPRESSED? Well, any of these labels can actually be introduced with a feeling in front of them I AM (feeling) TIRED, I AM (feeling) OVERWHELMED, I AM (feeling) SAD, I AM (feeling) DEPRESSED. The cool thing about the way we feel is that it's transitory: it comes and goes, as does our thinking state, because feeling and thinking are different sides of the same coin. So, we cannot BE our feelings as they come and go.

Our roles are similar. I used to see them as who I was and would wrap my being around them, especially the work role. When I moved to New York in 2005 to join my fiancé, my identity was so wrapped up in my work that I thought I was my work. Before leaving my job in Madrid, I was given the role of Exports Manager at a record label. This meant that I was the face of their international department and I was responsible for organising all of the fun events such as MIDEM and Popkomm, two major annual events for the music industry. It was an enormous responsibility to ensure that the international department was growing and progressing, and it really challenged me.

However, when I got to New York I was met with a very different scenario. As part of my master's in music business, I had to be an intern, which meant that I was in charge of making coffees and given a lot of admin tasks that were not challenging at all.

Because my identity was so wrapped up in my work and its labels, I soon felt really depressed and lost. I thought my self-esteem came from my label of exports manager, and I thought that without it I wasn't worth anything. As time went by, I realized that I didn't want to work for anyone else and I wanted to help others, so I decided to become a coach and help others to change their lives. However, the striving of making the business work would always get in the way of me enjoying the journey. When I started to get recognised by different publications and media for my book, I felt successful. But when I wasn't getting that attention, I felt unworthy and empty.

On Enoughness: We Are All Enough

I didn't feel enough. I don't know if you resonate with this. This feeling of **not-enoughness** can show up in many guises: in the form of people-pleasing, not putting boundaries where they are supposed to be, giving too much of oneself, not creating space for self-care or nurture, and not speaking up when you wish to. It takes many forms and guises, but these are just some examples that I have witnessed most among my clients. In short, this way of thinking causes us to shrink back and cower away from being the leader we were innately born to be.

What if you can feel enough right now? Because, in truth, you are more than enough; you always have been, and you always will be. Just because you don't know it now, doesn't mean you are not or that you won't see that you are in the future.

I really know this to be true for myself and everyone I meet. Why? Because I had a huge insight into this years ago when I was sitting in a field in Wales. I was minding my own business when, suddenly from nowhere, I heard a beautiful voice that came to me to share this very distinct message:

"If being is enough, I must be enough."

At the time, I was constantly in a space of striving, and for the majority of the time, I was dissatisfied with how I was feeling and the results I was getting. I suddenly felt a beautiful sense of peace and years of **not-enoughness** just fell away, and in its place I found a new experience of peace and a sense of freedom that I had only ever dreamed about.

What I have seen is, by our own innate capacity to have insights, our reality can change in a moment. And this is available to all of us. We all have the capacity for our stress, anxieties, and depressions to fall away and for us to live in the moment more of the time without actually doing anything unless it makes sense for you and I to do so. You don't need to discover who you are to be happy. Not knowing is just as delightful as you keep the mystery alive of who you are becoming along the way. You are built for love, kindness, compassion, and joy, so the foundations by which you were built are there to be enjoyed.

"If the only prayer
you ever say is
"Thank you,"
that will be
enough"

~ Eckhart Tolle

CHAPTER THREE

LIFE-LONG LEARNING JOURNEY

By Gretchen Phillips-Williams

As I look back through the years, I now see the errors in my ways. I do not have any regrets, but I do wish I had realized sooner the tremendous importance of love and gratitude and that it is necessary to continue honing these skills throughout our lifetime. I started strong, as I was fortunate to be born into a family that taught me about love and gratitude right from birth. My parents and large extended family have always shown me tremendous love and support. Through their endless examples and teachings, I learned early on that it is essential to be kind to others, to love your family, and to use your "pleases" and "thank-yous." These were my initial lessons in love and gratitude.

This solid foundation provided me with exactly what I needed as a child. Regardless, I recall the middle school years being somewhat turbulent; however, I believe this is quite common for that age. Girl drama is a real thing! By high school, I had learned it was best to leave the drama alone, and I found myself simply wanting to be friends with everyone. It was a very liberating time and, thanks to learning the importance of loving everyone, I have very fond, peaceful memories of high school. I continued this mentality as I graduated and became a young adult.

I assumed I had it all figured out and I was good to go. I graduated high school, started working full-time, was attending college full-time in the evenings, and lived on my own. After a couple of years, I decided I wanted to attend law school. I recall being very nervous the day I called and told my parents over the phone that my desire was now to attend law school and that, to do so, I would need to move home since the institution would not allow me to work full-time while a full-time law student. They agreed, and within a month I was moved out of my rental house and back into my parents' home. As difficult as it was to give up my independence of living on my own, I had made up my mind that law school was my next step and I was determined to make it happy. I was ecstatic to receive news of my law school acceptance and scholarship award on St. Patrick's Day! I was very grateful I had been accepted early to law school and that my parents were supportive. Life was good, and I was unstoppable…or so it seemed.

Shortly after starting law school, I met a guy that would play a significant role in my life. A week later, I badly broke my right hand while playing hockey. This made taking notes and writing law exams very difficult, as I was right-handed. Initially, I was determined to continue classes, but when the news came that I required surgery, it was recommended I take a medical leave. This was not at all how I had planned on law school going! I had met some fantastic new friends; I loved all of my law classes, everything was going exactly as I had planned until this! I was extremely disappointed, but the leave was necessary as I ended up needing three hand surgeries. I tried not to let the injury slow me down. I made the best of the situation by enjoying time with friends and dating the guy I'd met when I initially started law school.

Much to my surprise, while on break from law school, I fell in love and started seeing things from a "we" perspective rather than "I." After ten months of dating, we were engaged to be married. During this time, I decided I no longer wanted to become an attorney and take over the law firm I had been working for. I did not see that as working well for me as a wife and eventually a mother. Therefore, I opted not to return to law school, went back to finish my bachelor's degree instead, and was married after a short two-and-half-month engagement. My life had taken an unexpected new direction, but I was going with the flow and enjoying it.

Unfortunately, this was short lived. On our one-month wedding anniversary, my husband was involved in a severe accident. We were celebrating with our wedding party at an annual hayride event when it happened. What started as a happy celebration quickly turned into a nightmare. I now believe it was at this moment that I went into what I call "survival mode."

One minute my husband was joking around on the side of the moving hay wagon, and the next he was lying in the middle of a dirt road nearly immobile. I knew exactly what had happened the second it happened! I immediately jumped off the wagon, even before it stopped. No one else realized what the bump in the road had been, but I did! My husband had just been run over by a double-axle hay wagon loaded full of straw bales and people on a rural country road out in the middle of nowhere. It was pitch dark, but the headlight from the tractor approaching behind us provided just enough light for me to see him lying on his back in the middle of the road. I stood in front of him frantically waving my arms and yelling "stop."

My heart was pounding in my chest and I was fearful of what I was about to see. When the oncoming tractor had stopped, I then had to assess the situation. I am not sure how I knew what to do, but I sprang into action. He was conscious but in shock. It was apparent his right leg was severely broken. It was an open break, so there was blood coming through his jeans and staining the dirt below him. That was his only visible injury, but I knew there were likely additional internal injuries.

There was a great deal of panic among everyone there. I rallied our friends together so they could keep everyone away while the 911 call was made, and we waited for help. I refused to allow anyone to move him from the road, regardless of how much everyone wanted to do so. I stayed right at his head so he could see and hear me. I talked to him as calmly as possible. Someone brought over a blanket and we covered him. I stayed right there to be sure he stayed awake, still, and as calm as possible until the emergency vehicles arrived. There was mention of bringing in a helicopter, but they decided the ambulance could get him to the nearest trauma center in the same amount of time or less. I don't remember seeing the EMTs working on him or loading him into the ambulance. I had immediately moved out of their way to let them work, and the police and other emergency responders had lots of questions for me.

Regardless, I was not about to let him leave without me. We were miles away from where our vehicles were parked, so I rode in the front passenger seat of the ambulance. I vividly recall the ambulance stopping at an intersection so they could work on him. It was a very eerie span of time; it was as if time was standing still. I turned to see what they were doing, but I could not see into the back. I switched to listening. I could hear the EMTs' voices, but I didn't know what they were saying; however, I could sense the concern and urgency in their voices. The light at the intersection was flashing yellow and reflecting inside the cab of the ambulance. I was numb, just sitting there frozen, unable to do or say anything. I felt completely alone. Then suddenly we were moving again in a rush to get to the trauma center. I was separated from him as soon as we arrived at the ER.

It was not until I called his parents from the hospital emergency room that I burst into tears. How do you tell a parent that their child has been seriously injured? Tears rather than words flowed, I was eventually able to relay the news. After the phone call, I went to the restroom and regained my composure. I knew tears were not going to help the situation and that I had to be able to do whatever was necessary. It was there in that hospital waiting room, as I filled out numerous documents and waited hours for an update, that I was building a wall, a wall that I did not know about but something I felt necessary at the time. I was blocking out all the hurt, pain, and worry so that I could take care of business.

My new husband was very fortunate! He had internal bleeding and many broken bones, but he would live. After lots of tests in ER, he was taken into surgery to repair the open break to his tibia/fibula. He was placed in ICU after surgery recovery. I don't recall him being awake much while in ICU, but I do remember all the blankets over him, the tubes, the wires, and the beeping monitors. It was freezing in the room and the atmosphere had a heavy feel to it. While sitting in the corner of the ICU room, the fear of the unknown started to wander in, but instead of addressing it, I immediately raised the internal wall higher. I had no clue this was happening, nor did I know this wall would continue to grow stronger over the years and would end up having a very negative effect on my life.

After a couple of days, he was stable enough to be moved out of ICU and into a regular hospital room. The hospital room he was moving to was located at the end of a hallway. There was a small, hidden waiting area located outside the room's door. I was in this waiting area when the gentleman currently occupying the room was being moved out so that my husband could move in. The man was being transported to Mary Free Bed. He had recently been paralyzed from the waist down when he fell out of a tree while bow hunting. I recall observing this man lying in the hospital bed with minimal movement watching TV, always with a smile on his face. He was chipper and joking with the ambulance staff as they prepared him for transport and wheeled him down the hall. I did not know how to feel about this. I quickly dismissed it and moved on to the next task. It was a terrifying, overwhelming time of uncertainty, but I focused on whatever needed to be done and made sure it happened. I had become emotionally disconnected, but this seemed necessary at the time for me to keep on going.

Next on the list was my husband's second surgery to put his broken pelvis back together. Then there was ankle surgery, drain removal from his leg, continuing to work with the insurance companies and attorney, researching inpatient rehab facilities, trying to keep up my job, outpatient physical therapy research, and looking at our home to be sure it would be safe when he was finally able to return. There was always something more to be done. I was numb but very successful in getting everything completed.

My husband was finally able to return home. Upon discharge from rehab, he required outpatient physical therapy and he still had an external fixture holding his pelvis together. I was trained in pin care to clean those sites twice daily. He underwent a couple more procedures over the next few months to remove the fixture and to further fix his ankle. Thankfully, over time he fully recovered and was even able to return to his very physical job. The accident was quite a detour for us as newlyweds, but we continued as if nothing had ever happened, and then I was pregnant with our first child. At that point I had never considered the emotional impact the accident may have had on my young husband, nor did I realize the strength of the wall I had built within myself.

You get married, you have kids (before getting too old), you raise the children, work during it all, and live happily ever after. That was what I thought was expected, and it was my mentality, so it made perfect sense that we were now expecting a child. What did not make sense was our son arriving six weeks early. Perhaps it was a good thing I was still in survivor mode because this, too, was a challenging time. Giving birth in itself is an overwhelming, emotional process, but to then have your child rushed to NICU really takes it to a new level. Our son arrived before any of our scheduled birthing classes, so I was clueless and was not prepared to deliver, but I ignored all that and did what needed to be done. After delivery, he made no sounds. Just as I was starting to get worried, he finally cried. Then, as soon as he was stable, they moved him to NICU for further monitoring. I never shed a tear, never had a moment, I just carried on with whatever it was that needed to be done. Honestly, it was as if I was a robot.

Every day, I drove to the hospital and spent the entire day in NICU with our son. The elevator ride up to the unit was always the worst because there was nothing to do but stand there and wait and, well, I was not about to feel, so I would go through what needed to be organised when I arrived at the unit. You had to gain entrance, scrub in, place the fresh breast milk on top of his incubator, etc. Our son endured a couple of setbacks but was able to be discharged after two weeks. Again, life for my husband and me went on as if nothing had ever happened, but so much had happened!

This did not last long. Suddenly we were struggling with our marriage, or maybe just I was initially…I am not sure, but I am thankful for my survivor mode. It was up and down for a while, and then we separated when our son was about two years old. We lived separately for a couple of months until we decided to work it out and stay together. We sold the house he had bought just before we were married and made the decision to start over fresh in a new house.

Things seemed to be going well, and after a year I became pregnant with our second son. It was not a surprise pregnancy, but I'm not going to lie. My heart skipped a beat when the test showed positive, and I was initially hesitant to tell my husband. I was excited but also fearful of the unknown and how it might affect things. Many precautions were taken during this pregnancy to help prevent another early delivery. Regardless, we found ourselves rushing to the hospital five weeks early.

I was in the front passenger seat hoping I could make it to the hospital, and then my husband stopped at a red light. It was the same intersection where we had sat while in the ambulance after his accident. I know he had no idea, but I sure did. Once again, I was sitting there with everything out of my control. My contractions were only a couple minutes apart, but I was numb as we sat there. It felt like we were at that spot for a very long time; yet it went by in the blink of an eye. Next thing I knew we were at the hospital. I walked into the hospital, up the elevator, and right into a room where I delivered our second son within minutes of arriving. He was a premie, but he only required one extra day in the hospital, thankfully no NICU, and I am pretty sure my survival mode was in force.

Our married life continued as a family of four. I was a mom, wife, and full-time employee doing my best to make sure everything was complete and everyone had exactly what they needed. Only now do I realize that I was taking care of everyone except myself and that I was stuck in survivor mode. It had been five years since the accident, but I no longer knew any other way to live. The wall was high and strong at that point. I had become very accustomed to that mode. It mainly consisted of just doing what needed to be done and not talking about anything, especially emotions or feelings. It was just easier that way... or so I thought at the time.

Sadly our marriage came to a screeching halt when our youngest was almost two years old. Very little was ever said, but the children and I moved out and my husband and I divorced. I was angry, hurt, and very much still in my survivor mode, so I wasn't about to actually feel, express, or address any of those feelings. I immediately started dating because, at the time, I believed I needed to correct the situation. I was supposed to be happily married. I started talking to the very first man I met online, and in no time we were dating. This man was nothing like my first husband. As a matter of fact, he was a complete opposite. Just over a year later, against my parents' and friends' warnings, we were married.

This was the second marriage for both of us, but he had never had children, which he desired. I got pregnant right away and, before we knew it, our daughter was born. My second husband is a very good man. He treated my boys as if they were his and would do anything for his family. However, it was not too long after my daughter was born that I came to the realization I was still alone even though I was married. He traveled a great deal for work, and when home he was either on his computer or sleeping, which did not bother me since we were so different. I recall being in the backyard of the huge, new house he had just bought for us all and thinking, What have I done? I have a fantastic life and more stuff than I could ever want, but I don't have true love. I believe he loved me, but deep, deep down I was not truly in love with him the way I should be. I naturally thought I loved him or I would not have married him, but I had been in survival mode for so very long that I fear I had lost track of what real love was, and I had not allowed myself to feel in years.

I loved my three children without boundaries, but I didn't know if I could really love someone else. I recall thinking to myself; I need to stay for the kids; I need to stay, and it will all be fine. Well, I tried very hard to convince myself of this but could not. I knew it would be difficult for the children, but I also knew I could not remain married to this man. It was not fair to him, to the kids, or to me. I did not want my kids to grow up not knowing how to love genuinely. This was extremely difficult! I was slowly starting to see that feelings were necessary and essential, that I could not live a fulfilling life if I continued in survivor mode. I was learning that you have to feel to heal, and the truth was, I had not felt anything in a very long time.

This hit me like a brick wall. I could not believe I had messed up again. I was not supposed to fail, especially not twice! In an instant, my world was spinning out of control. I felt like I was having a nervous breakdown because, all of a sudden, I was attempting to deal with many years of built-up emotions. Eleven years is a long time to be in survival mode. I was starting to realize I had suppressed any problematic feelings or emotions to the point that, in some cases, I had completely blocked the memories. I had a couple of days where I did not want to get out of bed. It was awful. I felt like a complete screw-up, a horrible mother, and as though I had let everyone in my life down. I went from being the strong one to feeling as though I was broken into a million pieces.

I knew I needed help sifting through everything, so I started seeing a therapist. As soon as I started talking and feeling, things improved. I had no idea that, years ago in that hospital waiting room, I had begun building a wall and blocking out anything unfavorable.

My so-called survivor mode had become my norm and I had become a pro at sweeping the majority of my emotions under the rug. The relief I felt as I unloaded these items to the therapist was truly amazing. My therapy sessions consisted of me talking about how I felt about my current situation and then going back and discussing my feelings on all the past events I had endured. Through therapy, it also came to light that I had fallen out of love with myself. While in survivor mode I had forgotten about taking care of me. Knowledge is power, and now that I was aware of this, I could start doing something about it. I felt lighter and more full of life each time I left a therapy session.

During this time, I was going through a second divorce, starting over yet again, this time with three young children. I decided to move closer to my hometown so that I could be near my parents, family, and friends. I did not realize the magnitude of this at the time, but I had gotten too far away from what love really was and I needed desperately to find it again. Thankfully, I was slowly learning the necessary lessons, and I was not looking for love from someone else. Instead, I started doing stuff for me. I started doing light exercises, stretches, riding my bike, getting time with my girlfriends, having fun with my kids, and taking time for a bath. I had no interest in dating or being with anyone. To be honest, that was the last thing on my mind after two failed marriages. Instead, I was concentrating on my children and myself. I was falling in love with me again!

I discovered that my lack of being grateful for my feelings, emotions, and the awkward situations I came across led me to endure some tough times. Difficult times can always occur, but if we learn the lesson they are meant to teach and deal with them as they come up, then we can move forward. It is ironic to think I suppressed unpleasant emotions as an act of survival and, in doing so, I created more issues for myself. What I should have done was process each of the emotions/feelings as they arrived. As unpleasant as they may have been, they were there for a reason. I should have taken a moment with each emotion, shown it true gratitude for showing up and teaching me whatever it was there to guide me or taking me wherever it was meant to lead me, and then let it go. For example, the man being transported to Mary Free Bed, I believe he was just one of the many signs I ignored. I now believe the message there was be grateful, be very, very appreciative. Instead, I quickly dismissed the situation and tossed all of my feelings and emotions over a brick wall where they eventually became a raging fire.

Thankfully, I have learned that gratitude is essential, even of the most unwelcomed situations. It was not a natural process, but I had to pull down my wall, brick by brick, emotion by emotion, memory by memory. There is no longer a wall or a raging fire of fury. Instead, there is now a beautiful flame of love within me. Sometimes I have to remind myself of this, but I know it is there and I know love was the other missing part. I was not allowing myself to love out of fear of loss, and I had lost track of loving myself. However, love is the backbone of everything, and it starts within. If we truly love ourselves, we can then fully love others, as well as receive love.

As I continue to learn the importance of love and gratitude, I find myself more fulfilled than ever. I have lived a very blessed life, but in the past, I always felt as though something was missing. Who would have ever guessed it was me! Now that I am present, in love with myself and showing immense gratitude for both the good and the bad, the life I always dreamt of is showing up. I have an amazing fiancé. Our blended family of five children is perfect, and life is fantastic! I pray that I continue to learn and can pass these lessons on to my children. I want them to know that they need to express immense gratitude and love for everything and everyone, good and bad and that it is a life-long learning journey. Be present, be grateful, and love harder than you ever thought possible.

"Thank you for all the challenges
that built my character.
Thank you for all the hard times
that made me appreciate
the good times."

~Author Unknown

CHAPTER FOUR

LOVE AND GRATITUDE, THE ANTIDOTE TO MY DARKNESS

By Cheryl Maria Marella

Before I start my story, I want you to know that I don't blame anyone or any religion I mentioned in my story. Whatever I experienced in life was on me. And me alone.

The Intro

Hi, I'm Cheryl Marella. When I first got the text message asking me to contribute in this book, I thought, "Finally, I get a chance to share my story, and owning every bit of it - not just the glory, but also the shadows, the dark side and the scars as well.

I want you to know that I love everything I do and what I am today. I get to live the life I always wanted. My dreams are coming true one by one, and I am still excited for the future ahead. But it wasn't always like this.

The Battle

I was born an only child. My dad was a pilot and my mom's a doctor. I had my life handed to me on a silver platter. I had the job that most people dreamed of. I was a successful TV and Radio personality, I was ahead of Digital Marketing Team working for a High-End Mall in Jakarta, and I lived right in the heart of the city - a beautiful apartment on the 11th floor that I love. I always got invited to parties and events as a VIP, I was (and still am) well-connected to the people in my industry, and I have a great circle of friends. I went to one of the best Universities in Jakarta (UPH) and graduated in 3.5 years with perfect grades, I was dating popular guys and I always got what I want. My life was perfect, right? In no way to sound ungrateful, but if you answer 'yes' to this question, you are 100% wrong.

Let's go back four years ago. I woke up one morning in my apartment - my heart was racing, I couldn't breathe, and I was sweating heavily. My whole body was shaking, I was so scared and not really sure why. I was throwing up and crying, I couldn't bring myself to go to work, so I called in sick. I found out later that I was experiencing an anxiety attack. It became my ultimate battle.

But why? To answer this question, I will have to tell you the whole story. A story that I hope will inspire others to stay strong and love themselves before others. This is the one thing I learned later in life and I had to learn it the hard way.

My earliest memory of an anxiety attack was when I experienced a couple of bad incidents that happened all at the same time. One day I discovered a big secret about my Dad that almost ended my parents' marriage. It shattered my family apart. I was devastated, my mom was hurting inside, but she showed strength in front of me. We all went to family counseling, which I don't think helped. In the middle of this mess, I broke up with my then boyfriend of five years. He was heartbroken and was sent to a hospital one night because of the breakup. I saw him in pain and felt guilty. I don't deserve someone loving me because I will end up hurting them. At the same time, I was scared of being alone. I didn't want a relationship as it will end up being a mess like my family. I lost my faith in men at the same moment I lost faith in my Dad. But I also thought that without a relationship, how will I receive love? At the point, I already lost my confidence in deserving love cause I failed someone who loved me. This broken record kept playing in my head, and it created a series of anxious days and nights. But I never thought it would affect my life so much.

I was brought up in a strict religious Christian family. There were many limitations imposed on me by my family. One of them was, "You have to ask God before doing anything." For some people, this is a good thing. But I formed unassertiveness from it. I waited for approval from others before I did anything. I didn't believe in myself that I am capable of creating anything. There was no such thing as, "I can be, do or have anything I want." Because what if my desires don't align with God's plans? Then it's a sin, and I'm going to hell for it. I've been told that our focus is on the afterlife, that our present life is not that important. The focus is on going to heaven. So if this life isn't that big of a deal then, why bother doing anything? I was told that the purpose is to always be for the glory of God. But is it? How come I never felt that it is?

I had to sacrifice my life for religion. When I was a kid, my parents signed me up for extracurricular activities - Bali dancing and karate. I loved it. I got so excited to learn new dances, performing on stage, and doing sports. But one day, a family priest came into our house and told my parents that Bali dancing is a form of worshipping other gods and that's against God's will, so I had to stop dancing. He also said that Karate was violent and martial arts is using our own force rather than God's force. Needless to say, I had to stop Bali dancing and Karate. I didn't really want to, but it was because the priest said so. After that, I felt like walking on eggshells every day. My head was full of things that I shouldn't do because of the fear of God's wrath. After a while, I started to question it. Why would God give me things I love, to say no and take it away? What is my real purpose in life, because I don't think going to heaven is my ultimate goal. And for me to even question my belief, thinking that it could be wrong, made me feel guilty. I lived with the guilt for a while. I hated it and decided to run away from this religion mess to figure myself out.

I said goodbye to Jakarta and greeted New York City with open arms. No more religion or religious people, or so I thought. Also trying to find the real meaning of love. Didn't know that what you resist, persist. I briefly dated a guy I met in New York; he was a good-looking, fun, and smart Finnish guy. He was my classmate in acting school. He seemed like a normal guy at the beginning and he turned into a religious freak, after a few months, who cannot even be hugged because it was a sin. It happened in front of a subway station when we parted, I was about to go to class, and he was about to go back home. As I was about to hug him goodbye, he stepped back and said, "We can't do this anymore, we can't touch. God is the bride, and this can lead to sin." I felt like a huge brick was thrown to my head. What sin could we perform in front of New York City's crowded subway station? Hugging to say goodbye? I was angry and sad. I ran so far from home just to find someone exactly like what I ran away from. I felt abandoned and unlovable.

Abandonment. Not a strange word for me, unfortunately. With my Dad being a pilot he was always away, and Mom went to school overseas when I was six. I developed abandonment issues over the years. I discovered this after reviewing how I connected with people. I based all my relationship in life by being attached to people and hating them for leaving. My biggest fear is losing someone. I'm too scared to be alone. I always believed that people will end up leaving me. I didn't know how to survive on my own or that I am enough on my own.

I guess it's true what they say; you attract what you think. Due to my fear of loss and abandonment, people leave me. One of the saddest thing that happened to me was when my best friend stopped talking to me. She was someone I knew since I was six years old all the way until we were in our late 20s. I adore her so much, but it wasn't enough to make her stay. I was angry at that time. How could she do this to me? It wasn't until later that I found out from another friend that she was sick and tired of my complaining, insecurities, and just overall, an ungrateful person. My heart broke. It was a slap in the face. It hurt. It felt surreal being abandoned by someone who is close to you. And it wasn't just because she left, but also for the reason why she went. And again, I was left with the feeling of not being enough.

My life was basically a loop of questions I couldn't answer. What will I do next? Will I succeed? Am I good enough to do what I want to succeed or to survive? Would people love me? Would they hate me? How do I please everyone? Does he like me? Love me? Bored with me? These hot guys that were chasing me were the emotionally unavailable ones, but nobody knows that. I want to do more in the industry, but I didn't believe in me enough that I actually can, I always thought there's someone out there that is going to be better than me, so how long am I going to survive before that day comes and I will have no job? I want to do international shows, but then I doubted myself, what if my English isn't good enough? I'm an Asian girl, how the hell should I go about doing that? You can only see a few Asians who made it international, so my chances are thin. I felt powerless. Do I have to deal with this my whole life? It was the only thing I knew I was good at. And another 101 Questions in my head that I couldn't answer. 101 horror stories I created in my head of me failing, and it demotivated me every time. It created more anxiety. It was a vicious cycle. These questions add up to the whole, "I'm not enough and will never be enough." And the people around me didn't see this and the people that did, didn't have the heart to tell me because I always seemed happy with life.

I found another self-limiting belief I didn't realize I had for so long, "I have to be perfect to be loved." This belief came from work – entertainment. I was always judged by my look and performance. I had to always be perfect before anyone would love me or think I'm good enough. No wonder so many entertainers commit suicide, this is one of the hardest lines of work. It requires me to check back with myself all the time so that I don't lose myself in a mess. Also because I am the only child, my parents expect me to be perfect. As the eldest among my cousins, I was supposed to set an example. I shouldn't be caught doing anything bad, because then it will taint my reputation as well as my parents'. They're both successful doctors and pilots, so the bar was set high. Alongside with "I don't deserve to be loved," being perfect was added to my story - an impossible goal.

Years after years every time I accomplished something, in my head I was always doing it for someone else. For my parents, so they can be proud of me. For my boss, for my friends to like me, for the audience, for men to want to be with me, for my family to acknowledge me. The funny thing is, they were already satisfied with what I do, and it was just me that thought otherwise. I thought that if I achieved more, they would love me more. Not realizing that I was looking for love in all the wrong places.

So how did I numb the pain and void? I worked more and I worked harder. Did it help? For my career, yes, for my spirit and soul, no. Was I happy? Short-lived happiness, but mostly not. There was a hole in my heart. I didn't know what to do with it.

After a bad break up, and a series of anxiety attacks, I made a desperate move. I asked Google.

"What is wrong with me?"

I didn't expect that move to save my life. Not only did I find information about anxiety problems, but I found spiritual gurus and life coaches that helped me go through this journey of awakening. I had to take a 180-degree turn to change my mindset and fix my issues. And I have to start developing the necessary skill of self-love.

I remember one of the things my coach Tania told me, "Whatever you're trying to run away from will find its way to hunt you down. What you need is to find the root of this issue and make peace with it. And let love transform and heal you." This part required me to make an emotionally long distance phone call with my mom, and my dad to resolve the first layer of my issue. My mom couldn't stop crying. I told her I love her to death, and I respect what she believes, and that I see that it makes her a woman with a golden heart like she is. But it is not working for me. And that I hope she can be happy for me because I am happier now with my new beliefs. I don't hate Christianity, Jesus or the Bible. I respect them. It gave me a moral standard I needed growing up. I don't hate my mom either; she gave me what she thought was best for me. And I thank her for that. To me, religion is just an institution made by humans. So I don't do 'religion labels' anymore, but I still believe in God (that is within all of us) and Universe, and that I am (we are) the creator of our lives. I just let go of the limitation religion taught me.

I came to believe a new story that religion, whatever that is, as long as it makes you a better person, then it is for you. You can't force a belief to anyone, and all you can do is to accept the differences and coexist. Show love and compassion towards each other even though you have different views, race, and religion. And just because some religious people can be very frustrating, they're the people who misunderstand what religion is about, doesn't mean all of them are. People forget that religion is about love, compassion, and acceptance instead of judging. It's the small bunch of people who end up being terrorists, extremist and murderers who got it all wrong, not the religion itself. Those are the new beliefs I developed. It was liberating to free myself from the old frustrating belief and to walk confidently towards love and self-growth.

Fast forward to three years later, I was filming for a documentary in Surabaya, at Church GKI Diponegoro that was bombed by Muslim extremist last May 2018. I was standing right where the three female underage bombers died. It was about ten days after the incident. The church was operating again. I was staring at the sunrise, listening to the gospel songs sung by people inside the church. 100% of them said they forgave the bomber, and that they are not afraid. I had that warm feeling in my heart, a reminder of how peaceful Christians and Catholic are even in dark times. I felt peace. No more resentment towards them, and strangely, I felt compassion towards the bombers. This wound is healed.

I also talked to my dad one day, telling him honestly how he made me feel, trying to understand where he is coming from, why he did what he did, also giving forgiveness. Seeing him full of compassion and from the eyes of source. It created a space for us both to have a better father-daughter relationship, to be best friends, travel partners and to be family, rather than enemies. Our relationship slowly recovered. As well as our whole family. We even went for a weekend trip to Thailand together, just the two of us!

I also made peace with the fact that I lost a best friend. As much as it was difficult for me to let go, I had to tell myself that if I had to lose her, I believe something good will come after this experience. I don't hate her for that; if I were in her shoes that time, honestly, I might feel the same way about me. In fact, subconsciously, I don't think I even liked me back then either. I hope wherever she is right now; she is living a happy life.

"Love yourself and you can heal your life" – Louise Hay.

All of my issues above - the anxiety, abandonment, feeling unlovable and not good enough, can be cured with love. I understand it now. I know now that to be loved, I have to love myself first. For me not to feel abandoned, anxious and not good enough, I have to know my value, and that I deserve the best. For me to attract all that in my life, I have to be all that for myself first.

I'll strive to be the best version of myself every day.

After I decided to take on this journey with an open heart, I've made a pact with myself that I will be strict with myself going through this process. I am determined to be happier. I only have one goal, and that is to be happy. I started to list down my strengths and the things that I love doing. I started doing them to boost my mood. I began to list down what I appreciate about myself; then I do self-care. I began to take care of me (Body, mind and spirit).

Body:

I take my time every day to look at myself in the mirror, look at myself in the eyes and tell myself, "I love you, I love your shape, I love your face, I love your smile." I started to love my flaws, my skinny petite body, my freckles, my breakouts (I don't go out with makeup anymore and very confident about it), my nose, lips and forehead that I used to think was too big. At least that was what my friends back in junior high told me and I believed them. But not anymore. I love every inch of my body. And I work out, I sweat, I do yoga or any sports, I eat healthier food, drink more water, and all these are my self-love acts. I appreciate me, to the point where I don't care anymore if people would like me because I like me. I love me and that's enough. The more I love myself, the less anxious I am, and I almost don't care about my abandonment issues. I managed to be strong in my core now, I know my value, and I know people will and do love me too. I don't need to be scared of losing anyone anymore.

"Gratitude is the way to bring more into your life"
– Abraham Hicks.

Mind:

I promised myself I will not feed my mind with bullshit anymore. I said goodbye to super mellow songs, angry rap songs, and any song that can trigger negativity. I said goodbye to horror movies that inflicted fear. And I started to read, watch, and listen to things that lifted my spirit. I trained my mind to focus on positivity instead of negativity. I strengthened my mind to believe that everything is always working out. I trained my mind to see the beauty in everything I see.

I started to make a list of what I love and be grateful about what is, about Jakarta, my country, my work, my friends, my family and my pets, and looking at life from a different perspective. Focusing on the things that are working and making me happy, made me happy. Not just gratitude, but now I can be satisfied with what I have right now and enjoying myself being in the moment.

Spirit:

I learned meditation. I do it morning and night. Focusing on my breathe and reaching the stillness of the mind. This part helped reduce my anxiety attacks. The calmer I am, the stronger I can feel my intuitions. The more I operate from a place of love. The more I grew faith in myself, the more loving I became. I also write and listen to a lot of positive affirmations. I do this when I wake up and before I sleep, and even though I fall asleep while listening, my subconscious will still catch and record it. That is my favorite exercise.

But this is not as easy as flipping the palm of your hands. There are loads of ups and downs. You have to heat and melt gold before shaping it into a piece of jewelry, right? The process is painful, uncomfortable, and requires me to open up, be vulnerable and honest with myself. It requires me to point out and face my biggest fears, to be aware of what I think and what I feel, knowing they're my point of attraction. And to start operating with love as the source, instead of fear.I might have to live for the rest of my life with those issues; I don't mind it now. For me, as long as I'm aware of what's going on in my head, I can always control my mind and I will know how to tame my inner demons.

The Now

As I began to embrace love and gratitude, my confidence grew. I love myself and I can love others. I have loads of love to give to any living being in this world. I have a strong mind and I began to attract the things and the life I wanted. Now I'm doing a documentary project with a Singaporean TV Station (details are still confidential, but my desire to do TV Hosting for an international media came true) after leaving CNN Indonesia. I coach people in Public Speaking, I have a show on 87.8 HardRock FM Bali, and a department head for GOJEK Newsroom. Also, I've been seeing an amazing man. Life is so good.

Before flying back to Indonesia to move to Bali, Tania, my coach asked me the ultimate question, "Have you found your purpose in life?" My answer was, "Yes, I will inspire people with love to do the things they love, to love themselves, and to love their lives. From now on I'm a love warrior. And I am grateful to everyone that's been on my journey, to my parents and family, and friends, and on top of all, to myself. I wouldn't have done this without me."

"I'm thankful
for my struggle
because without it
I wouldn't have
stumbled across
my strength"

~ Alex Elle

CHAPTER FIVE

LIFE-BUILDING DREAMS

By Leanne Cordova

What If I fall? Oh, but my darling, what if you fly?

I have been on a path of self-development and learning for the last ten years. Over this time, I have had to face what felt like the scariest thing to date: to trust myself and embrace love. Not from others, as that would later come, but from myself. To truly, without judgment—love myself—not accept who I was, but to embrace who I was and love myself for it. For all my scars and past decisions, for all the guilt I carried and how I allowed myself and others to be treated. To develop into the beautiful, caring woman and mother, I am today—the tenacious, determined, inspired woman with drive to learn and better myself—the mother and wife who provides support and unconditional love, supporting the journeys of others and encouraging them to always do their best and strive for more.

To understand my journey and what led me to feel loved, and to be able to give the gift of unconditional love to others, you first need to understand who I was before I got here.

I was the youngest of four kids growing up in your standard family upbringing. My dad worked hard to support us financially, and my mum spent her days looking after us four and working.

I remember always feeling alone. Not in a sad way, that nobody loved me and didn't give me enough attention: it was more like I was alone in my being, as I didn't need anyone. I was very independent from a young age and knew what I did and didn't want. I saved from an early age, and when I was 14 years and nine months old, I had myself my first job. I loved working, as it allowed me the independence to make my own choices, and I knew that when I finished school and started working full-time, I would not rely on any man or person to look after me. This is what drove me for so many years, as I didn't want to end up like Cinderella or Snow White who needed rescuing by Prince Charming.

I never felt like I needed someone else to feel okay, to feel wanted or included. However, this did make me feel like I never really belonged anywhere. Growing up through high school, I didn't fit into any one group; I loved sport, art, maths, cooking, metal work…to name a few. My closest friend and I would bounce from group to group, depending on how we felt on the day. Sometimes I'd hang out with the kids that would get stoned at lunch, other times with the kids that loved sport or IT, and sometimes on my own in the art room.

This was okay with me, as I liked the variety of interacting with so many diverse people with different goals and desires in life or lack thereof.

Throughout my teenage years, I seemed to attract the guys that always needed fixing. I always found myself trying to see the beauty in everyone and would help them to see it within themselves, to see their self-worth and ultimately the desire to be better than they were. I remember one guy I was seeing, unbeknown to me at the time, was associated with a known Melbourne gang and was doing copious amounts of drugs while we were together. I always knew something didn't feel right about him; however, I was young and naive and just wanted to believe that with love and understanding everyone can be better, not realising that maybe not everyone wants to grow and be more than they are.

Later I met someone who was lively and outgoing, and things felt new and exciting. I was studious and diligently working my way through promotions in the bank, and he was a forklift driver who worked nights, listened to loud music, and dressed as a punk with the typical punk hairstyle. Our opposite worlds attracted us, and within a few years of knowing each other, we were blessed with a beautiful baby boy. I struggled being home in that first year, coming from the career world of being goal-orientated, money-driven, independent and striving for my next raise to the role of a stay-at-home mum with this little baby that cried (what felt like) all the time. He fed between two to four hours for the first six months and slept maybe two hours at a time if I was lucky. He was unsettled most of the time unless I was holding him. Years later, I discovered that the negative interactions surrounding his father and me played a big part in this.

I was only 23 and this parenting stuff was so unfamiliar to me that I felt my world getting smaller by the day. I was exhausted, sleep deprived, and I felt trapped like a prisoner in my own home which I was unable to escape from. I had a constantly crying child needing love and safety from his mum, and I struggled to find it within myself to give to him.

I felt like I was an empty shell, and I wasn't present. My mind would escape, and I just went through the motions of life, not living, just being.

It got to a point where I was so unhappy, and, if I had to label it, I would call it postnatal depression. I remember vividly the day I begged my son's father to stay home and not go to work, as I was so scared of what I might do to him. I loved him so much, but I just didn't trust myself with him. His father brushed this off and went to work, and funnily enough, went out drinking with a mate that night, as apparently he, too, needed time out. Our relationship was never a great one, to begin with; it was volatile and unsupportive, and on occasions, I felt threatened by him.

Over time, I considered leaving him, but I didn't think it was possible. It's funny how our unconscious beliefs actually influence our decisions without us realising. And it may just be something we heard when we were younger, something which has sat dormant in our beliefs all this time, waiting to arise when we need to utilise it, whether it is beneficial or not.

I believed there was no way out from this relationship, that I had committed to having a child with this man and I had to be with him forever. If I were to leave, it would be disapproved of by others and bring shame upon myself. The saddest part is, I really believed the only way out of this relationship was when I died, and I started looking forward to my death and even contemplating suicide. It sounds ludicrous, I know, but at the time I honestly believed this was the only way out. I had become a shadow of the person I once was.

I went back to work part-time, which helped increase self-worth, significance, and desire for living. However, I still wanted more than this life. I still felt trapped.

We both wanted to travel Australia and see more of what our beautiful country has to offer, and I was sick of being the sensible one in the relationship: always watching what we spent, ensuring the bills were paid first and that my partner's and son's needs were taken care of before my own. Before having my son, I had worked and saved persistently for five years, and I had kept a large sum of money. With this money, we purchased a 40-foot bus that had been converted into a motorhome, with the plans of working and travelling. We planned to have another child during our travels and found out I was pregnant within the first cycle of trying.

I was so excited about the prospects of our growing family and our upcoming travels that it's probably fair to say I wasn't living in reality and chose not to focus on the growing amount of problems we had between us. All this was very short-lived, and reality set in within a month when I realised I was excited about everything other than the partner I had chosen to spend my life with. I had overlooked this slight detail because it was easier than facing the truth. However, the gnawing and constant dread inside of me wouldn't subside, and I knew if I didn't make this decision, as hard as it was, I would find myself in some remote part of Australia with just the four of us and our problems. This scared and unnerved me so much that I decided to face my fears and leave.

It was possibly one of the hardest decisions I have ever made, but one of the easiest to follow through with once I had decided. My ex-partner and I no longer loved each other, and we were ultimately staying together for the love of our children. I had reached my threshold and I was no longer okay with being yelled at, put down, and stood over by someone with the intention to threaten and intimidate me. The constant mind games and fear were draining me physically and emotionally. I had realised I could not bring another child into this world where the emotional abuse would appear as normal behavior. I did not want to raise my two beautiful caring boys up in a relationship which would inevitably lead them down the track to becoming abusive, domineering men with little respect for the women in their lives.

If I were to say the separation was easy, I would be lying. It made me grow and develop in ways I('d) never expected. I was pregnant, working, looking after our three-and-a-half-year-old son, and homeless temporarily. My beautiful sister opened her home up to us, where we stayed until I had secured a rental property six weeks later. I worked up until the end of my pregnancy and then took maternity leave when our adorable second child was born.

This was when my real growth started to blossom.

Looking back, now I can appreciate the pain, torment, hatred, sadness, and heartache that surrounded me, as well as the emotional and psychological abuse I'd received multiple times a day for years. It led me to choose differently for myself and my family. It taught me to trust myself and my instincts, to be grateful, and—most importantly—to love and give love freely.

My boys' father and I could not agree on custody arrangements, and we spent a lot of time in mediation and, finally, court. Court is a horrible process where the creativity of story-telling seems to shine, and you may find yourself defending claims that are entirely mythical, although the ownership is on you to prove they are false. Going through this process ignited courage and strength in me; however, it also created hatred and anguish for what is unjust and wrong with humankind.

Our boys continued to grow and spend time with us both separately, and it was in these days and nights while they were away that the realisation of how lonely I was began to emerge.

Going through the separation seemed to create an invisible barrier between myself and others. Not all, but some friends and family seemed to keep at a distance. I don't think it was a conscious thing. Over time I have come to understand that people seem to find it challenging to understand divorce, and I think it becomes too real for them, maybe highlighting things in their own lives, so they keep away. I was also finding it difficult to be around men in general, as I had developed an image of them as being untrustworthy and dangerous.

At one family function, I was purchasing a drink from the bar when a young guy said hi to me. I looked at him and froze. My body language became rigid and uninviting. I hadn't noticed until my brother, who was standing on the other side, asked what was wrong with me, pointing out that the guy had innocently said hi.

It made me realise that more than being scared of men, I didn't trust myself and my, as I thought my last decision hadn't turned out so well. This was the turning point for me. I knew that, unless I wanted to be on my own forever and be stuck in limbo, I needed to work this stuff out and heal myself.

I searched online for meetups and found myself being attracted to a hypnotherapy/NLP course.

On gut instinct, I attended the meetup which, in turn, led me to sign up for one of their 10-day courses. This was a massive stretch for me, as I had never flown anywhere on my own before, and I was due to fly interstate in six-weeks' time. I knew it was a risky decision. My boys had I had never been apart for more than a few days, and now I didn't have a babysitter or accommodation, I knew nothing about this company, and it was a substantial investment. They promised that they could help me, and deep in my soul, I believed they could.

It was through this amazing experience that I was able to release so many toxic emotions which were holding me back and clouding my ability to make sound decisions. I was able to uncover past abuse from an extended family member. I hadn't realised how much this incident had shaped my choices up to this moment. I allowed myself to feel—to feel emotions that I hadn't experienced in years, and maybe never.

I felt the world being lifted off my shoulders and began to experience feelings of being connected—really connected—to myself and others around me. This block I had carried around with me for so many years was now gone, and it felt amazing.

I continued my emotional growth over the months and years that followed. Self-doubt and insecurities gave way to self-worth and confidence. Understanding replaced judgemental thoughts and love dispelled hatred. I was safe to embrace the person I had always been: loving and caring.

I once read this book about a relationship being like boats. The boat is a metaphor for each individual, and on the external and internal you may have some dints and marks from previous life experiences and relationships. However, you are floating on the water, some looking better than others. When you spend time with another person, would you allow them to take a sledgehammer to your boat and make holes in the side so that you start to take on water and ultimately sink? Or would you want them to treat your boat with respect and maybe even help you make some repairs?

This metaphor has remained with me, and I feel profoundly connected to it.

I was ready for an intimate relationship, and I wanted to attract a partner with a similar mindset: that a relationship is about helping and encouraging each other to grow in whichever way we desire, to help each other become better and enjoy this time together. And if our paths happen to separate, we must know we will both be okay to continue our journeys, as we have taken care of our own boats.

I wanted to connect with someone on a more emotional and romantic level, and through mutual family members, I was introduced to a beautiful soul.

He was patient and caring and loving. He accepted my need for space as an individual and as a mother and tried his best to understand when I would push him away if I felt things were moving too quickly. I was mindful of not wanting to lose myself in another relationship. He also understood and respected my decision to not introduce the children to him until I was ready, dating for six months before I even mentioned his name to the boys. For the patience and love, he shared with me over this time, I am forever grateful.

While enjoying our new relationship, we become aware we were both carrying emotional baggage that was no longer serving us. He saw the changes I was making in myself and thankfully saw the value in us as a couple, and for his self-improvement, he has been on a journey of learning, self-development, and healing alongside me. The continual growth between us has been the pinnacle ingredient in our commitment to each other and is why we choose to be in a relationship together every day.

Over the years that followed, my partner, my boys, and I have learned to create a new family dynamic that is unique to us. My partner is learning to be a father, and I applaud his effort, as it couldn't be easy coming into a new relationship with little children. My boys have learned to embrace new ways of thinking and the flexibility to move between two very different worlds on a continual basis. They are learning to love themselves and shine their lights bright, even when others may try to diminish them. They are the best teachers a parent can have and are my drive for constant improvement. I am forever grateful for the journey we have shared, for the love they have given me, and for the handsome young men they are.

It is easy to get caught up in the mundane activities of life and make excuses for being too busy to connect with family and friends. In the past, I have had a habit of doing this, and I am striving to improve each passing week by being present and setting aside time to enjoy the now.

My oldest son is a sport fanatic, who has speed, dexterity, and determination. He loves his footy and plays for our local team on Sundays. As a family, we set aside the day each week to watch and encourage him from the sidelines. To be a part of his passion and see him shine doing something he loves is priceless and something I will always cherish.

My youngest son is highly creative and always busy constructing something. He has the mind of an engineer, always wanting to discover how things work. I remember the first time he went on a Ferris wheel, and while everyone else looked out at the scenery, he was watching the cogs go round and round, working out the mechanics of it. He has gone from strength to strength recently with his swimming, facing his long-running fear of placing his head in the water to swimming like an awe-inspiring dolphin. I was brought to tears only weeks ago while watching him jump from the deep end into the water, his fear now a thing of the past.

The times we spend together as a family can vary from month to month, although the top activities generally include day trips, playing games, and cooking yummy food. I'm quite fond of lying in bed with the boys and reading a book together or being active with them at the park or something similar. My partner, on the other hand, does a fantastic job of getting into character with the boys. They have a fun game where he will leave a nerf gun at the front door with instructions for them to find him if they dare. Another hit with the boys is where they all dress up in their wrestling costumes (which generally consists of undies, headbands, ripped singlets, sunglasses, etc.) and they each wrestle for the opportunity to win the championship belt.

We come together every night to share a family dinner at which we each contribute stories of our day and what we have learnt. Sometimes it might be the quirky science facts or disturbing documentary tales, what we have done at work or just something that we have enjoyed or something that even upset us.

Nonetheless, my favourite time with these three special people is Friday nights, which is also known as movie night at our house. We get the doonas out and snuggle on the couch with some yummy food. I get to be close with them all and enjoy their cuddles, talking about our week and chilling with a movie on. These moments are so precious to me.

To be able to embrace love and gratitude is a freeing experience, and I aim to accept others for where they are. It's not always easy, as I don't always understand where they are coming from, but I make a conscious choice not to judge. I honestly believe we are all doing the best we can with the knowledge we have available to us.

At 36 years young, this journey has taught me to be courageous and resilient, to face the unknown with strength, to trust my instincts and welcome healthy boundaries but, most importantly, to always have love in my heart and understanding without judgment for where someone is at this moment in his life.

My journey has guided me through a place of self-discovery where I now feel safe, loved, and centred. My childhood and friendships, my relationships—and all the bits in between—have helped lead me to a place of understanding. Understanding and acceptance of myself and others: for this, I am truly grateful.

As I look back at everything I have accomplished and forward to what my future may have in store,

I become excited about all the possibilities of what I can achieve in the coming years. I have a desire to help as many people as I can to feel empowered to follow their dreams. I am fortunate that my online business has given me the capacity to help others through sharing my journey and life lessons. I am grateful to inspire others to have the courage and desire to grow, to lead themselves and increase their financial wealth so as they can live the life of their dreams.

"Give thanks for blessings every day. Every day. Embrace gratitude. Encourage others. It is impossible to be grateful and hateful at the same time."

~ Denzel Washington

CHAPTER SIX

THE JOY OF MOTHERHOOD

By Fernanda Lorenti

"I am sorry, your daughter will never walk again." The doctor said to my parents.

I was an active child, but I found myself in a wheelchair at the age of 14, caused by an adverse reaction to a polio vaccine. Despite the doctor's prognosis, I beat the odds. Two years after I started walking again, I ran a five-kilometer race and won first place.

Throughout my life, I have been able to overcome many challenges, with a deeply held faith that I could move mountains if I needed to, and especially if I believed that I could. I survived a car accident that put me in a coma on my 21st birthday and the doctors told my family that they did not think I was going to wake up; yet, once again, I did what they said could not be done.

As a result of my experiences, I have learned that you should never allow people to tell you how they think your life is going to be. Anything is possible if you believe it in your heart and your soul. We can make things happen even when no one believes it is possible. I've learned that life can end at any minute, so it is imperative to live every single moment to the fullest—to love myself, my life, and everything in it. I've learned to not take anyone or anything for granted and to always be extremely grateful because we don't know if we will have tomorrow; we only have right now.

So, I started doing everything that I loved. I began to study everything I could about human psychology and the functions of our brain. I shared what I was learning with others so I could help them have happier, more fulfilled, and more productive lives. I was manifesting many of my desires and achieving my biggest dreams, using all of the tools that I was learning about. Some of the manifestations happened quickly, like finding the perfect parking spot every time I needed one; and some took a little longer, like traveling the world and getting paid for it. I always felt happy, blessed, and grateful, even when life was challenging and full of not-so-good surprises, because, in my heart, I knew that everything was going to be fine in the end—that is, until one day, when my faith was shaken.

I was living the life! I had an amazing career doing what I loved, I was married to the man I loved, and I was ready to manifest one of the biggest dreams of my life—to be a mom. I always saw myself in this big house surrounded by many kids, playing and having fun; and I could not wait to see this dream become a reality. Soon after my husband and I got married, we were ready to have our baby, and we started trying. A few months of trying to conceive turned into a few years, and sex turned into a chore—an obsession to become pregnant. Every month, I was making sure it was on the right days, feeling excitement that would inevitably lead to anxiety after finding out that we had failed again. It was devastating and sad. Whenever I saw a mother with a baby in her arms, or a family with many kids, I was happy for her, and at the same time, so sad for myself that tears well up in my eyes.

Physically, everything was fine with my body. The doctors were telling me that I should get pregnant at any time. I was using all the tools I had learned on how to manifest what I desired for my life, yet the most important dream of my life was not happening the way I had planned. What was I doing wrong?

After years of trying to get pregnant, life became different. It was hard to keep a happy face—to look at myself in the mirror month after month, not seeing any positive results. I couldn't help but feeling like I was a failure. On the occasions when my period was late, I would run to the drug store, buy a pregnancy test with my heart filled with hope and excitement, only to find myself crying on the bathroom floor with a negative test result in my hands. I cried myself to exhaustion, leaving just enough strength to crawl into bed and sleep. My relationship with my husband at that time had also changed. It was hard to keep the passion when we were both so focused on getting a positive result. We tried virtually everything: eating the right foods, not eating the wrong foods, wearing the right men's underwear, so his little fellas were not too constricted, taking the right supplements, having sex in the right positions…anything and everything to make for a more relaxed swim. And let's not forget to keep the legs up so gravity can do its part! You name it, we tried it all, and nothing worked.

Christmas was the hardest time for me. It is my favorite time of the year, seeing all of the families together, the kids playing with their parents, opening their gifts with big smiles on their faces. I always loved it, and I wanted to share that experience with my children. I wanted to have my own family and to do all those things—decorating the Christmas tree together, singing songs, baking cookies, buying their favorite toys and watching their faces light up as they opened their presents in the morning.

I was born and raised in Brazil, which is where my family was living while I was in the USA with my husband. We celebrated Christmas every year with his family at their home, and those years that we were trying to conceive were not comfortable. I was feeling that I was losing hope and that I was not going to be able to have my own family. I felt entirely alone and sad for not being able to get pregnant, and I missed my family. To make matters worse, I found out that my husband's mom and sister were telling everyone that I did not want to get pregnant because I did not want to get fat.

They were never happy that my husband chose to marry someone that was not an American. They considered me too happy, too skinny, and too positive. His mother told me once at a Thanksgiving dinner party that being a loving and happy wife to her son was not that important; what mattered was that I had not given him a child. Her daughter had given her four grandchildren already, but that didn't lessen the pressure that she was putting on me to conceive. I held my tears to the end of the party since my way of being is always to show a happy face when in public and keep my sadness and sorrows for when I am alone; but on that day, I could not hold my tears for very long. As soon as I got to the car, I cried. I never said anything to them about how I felt about their comments about me. I was in a different country with an entirely different culture—I just wanted to be loved and accepted. At the time, I did not know how to establish boundaries and earn respect. I have since come to understand that if you allow people to disrespect you once, they will take over your life, and by the time you realize what has happened, you will be caught up in their games not knowing what to do. Through that situation, I learned that it is never too late to start establishing boundaries., no matter who's involved.

Then one day, I realized that with all that was happening in my life, I had completely withdrawn from my faith. I was so disconnected from my spiritual practice and my soul. So I went within and started reconnecting with my soul, my inner self, and with God. Through my meditations and prayers, I realized that God knew better. I needed to release the sadness from my heart and to surrender to the situation that I was going through and allow God to take over. Instead of focusing on what was not happening in my life, I decided to focus on what I was grateful for, all the good things that were happening, all the people who loved me and cared for me. I started writing a journal. I call it my gratitude journal. I started writing about all the great things I was blessed with in my life. (I still have it and write in it every night.) Little by little, I was able to feel happy and loved again. I began to do the things that I loved to do and living my life to the fullest. My husband and I went on date nights and we started having fun, reconnecting with each other on a deeper level, and more. I was learning to make lemonade from the lemons life was throwing at me.

A few months into my journey of self-discovery, I heard clearly in meditation that for me to have a child, I needed to do in-vitro fertilization (IVF). When my husband came back home that night, I discussed it with him and we decided to look into it. We started doing research and made an appointment with a very well-acclaimed fertility doctor to inquire about the procedure. After many exams, we found out what was happening to us and why we were not getting pregnant. In-vitro was our only chance to get pregnant since his sperm was not strong enough to perforate the eggs on their own.

At last, hope was restored in my heart and I could see the light at the end of the tunnel. My prayers had been answered and I could see and feel myself becoming a mom from that moment on. Both scared and excited, we started the process. On the day after Christmas of 2004, I decided to do some after-Christmas shopping to buy some decorations with my sisters-in-law. I was at one of the stores when I saw this cute green Christmas sock ornament with the name Michael on it. I picked it up, then I turned to my sister-in-law and said to her, "This is my first present for my son. He is coming soon, and his name will be Michael." I knew in my heart and soul that what I was saying to my sister-in-law at that moment was going to happen. After window shopping for some hours, we went back home.

After a few months of intense IVF treatment, my husband and I went to the fertility clinic to do the final pregnancy test. My heart was filled with joy because even though the trial had not been done yet, I could already feel my son's heart and soul in my belly, and of course, there was still one part of my mind that was doubting if it was real. "Will I be able to conceive?" I just decided to ignore the doubting voice and listened to my heart. We did the blood test and waited for the result, which would be ready in a few hours. We had a meeting with one of our clients, so we drove to our client's home praying that this time we were going to be able to have a baby. Can you imagine how our hearts were beating while waiting for the doctor's call? Staying focused on our presentation to our client was not easy since we were both looking at our phone every single minute awaiting the call that was going to change our lives—the call that was going make us the happiest people on Earth.

We told our client that we needed to leave our phones on and if we received a call, we would have to answer it immediately. During the middle of the presentation, after looking at my phone for the hundredth time, it finally rang and I grabbed the phone in my hands. My hands were shaking and my heart was beating so strong and fast that you could probably hear it from a distance. I wanted to know what the result was but was also afraid of getting bad news. With a trembling voice, I answered, "Hello, this is Fernanda," and the lady on the other end of the line said, "Congratulations, you are going to be a mom!" I cried with so much joy. My husband was sitting right next to me; he held me in his arms, we cried and prayed together with so much gratitude in our hearts for the most amazing gift that a human being could ever receive. I don't remember how because my head was in the clouds, but I think we finished our meeting with the client and went out to celebrate the new life that was about to come into our lives.

About three months later, I started feeling pains in my stomach one afternoon and discovered that I was bleeding. I was so afraid; I began to cry and I started talking to my son. I told him that he was a strong boy and pleaded for him to hang on. I made promises to him and said to him that everything was going to be ok, and I prayed to God for a miracle. I called my husband and he quickly took me to the hospital, only to find out that it was a minor issue and that the baby and I were going to be fine. During the pregnancy, I was so happy. I spoke to little Michael every day, played classical music for him, reminded him of how much I loved him already, how amazing and loved he was by all. I was the happiest pregnant mom ever; the more prominent and rounder I became, the happier I was.

Time went by and I was due for delivery. We had planned a natural birth, but since I was tiny, little Michael was having a hard time coming out and was getting stuck. My fantastic doctor opted for a cesarean section, and in less than ten minutes, Michael was out. He did not cry right at the moment he came out, so the doctor, nurses, and beautiful angels quickly moved little Michael to a nearby table so they could clean his lungs, and then I finally heard my baby's crying song. On December 7, 2005, at Beverly Hills Hospital, in a room which had a window view of Hollywood's big, famous sign, an angel came to this earth to share his love, kindness, and wisdom with us. My amazing son.

When he started to cry at the nurse's care, I said, "Michael, mommy is here." Immediately, he turned his head towards my direction and stopped crying. Everyone in the room was amazed that he recognized my voice right away and it made him calm.

We were decorating our Christmas tree at home a few weeks later, and I remember hanging his little green sock ornament with his name on it. I can't even describe how grateful I felt at that moment. I knew that my love for my son would be significant, but the love I was feeling was utterly indescribable. It was and is the most beautiful, unconditional love that one human being can feel for another.

Today he is 12 years old, and he is an example of love, happiness, respect, kindness, intelligence, and wisdom in everything he does. When he was only five years old, I lost my father. I was in the USA and my father was in Brazil. I was talking with my sister over the phone and she shared with me the news about my father's death. As I started to cry, my son Michael came to me, hugged me, looked me in the eyes, and said, " Mommy, he is in a much better place right now and he is happy." This 5-year-old boy's words gave my heart so much peace and understanding. Because of his words, I was able to have a clear, peaceful mind to handle all the arrangements.

I needed to travel to Brazil that same day to say goodbye to my Dad before he was buried. In Brazil, the family only has 24 hours from the moment the person dies to the moment the person needs to be hidden. I was able to be with my father for two hours before it was time. This was one of many magical moments that my son and I have shared, and he continues to share his wisdom with me. He has this amazing, beautiful, old soul, and we have an incredible connection that's always filled with love, kindness, laughter, honesty, and respect for each other.

He is learning how to make his own choices in life. He loves soccer, and it is his true passion. He knows exactly what he wants for his future, and the big smile on his face is his signature of life and I am so proud to be his mom. Every day, we make sure to laugh a lot, and we are always silly with each other. Each night, we share at least the three surprising things that happened to us that day and discuss what we are most grateful for. We always remember to learn and focus on our blessings and on what we have instead of what we don't. From the day he was born, I've held my son in my arms and told him how much I love him, how amazing he is, how he can be and do anything in his life, and that he is a champion. I am forever grateful to have him in my life. He is the most beautiful gift of love that God shared with us. My heart leaps with joy every moment that I see or think about my son. One of the greatest feelings a woman can have is the joy of motherhood.

"When I started counting my blessings my whole life turned around."

~ Willie Nelson

CHAPTER SEVEN

SMALL WINS

My approach to connection, redefinition, and holding space

By Manal Akkad

There was a time when I'd open my eyes to the feeling of dizziness, headache, and pounding heart, wondering if tomorrow it was going to stop, go away, or haunt me forever. Every day for about two years, I questioned how it had gotten that far and wondered if there would be a turning point. I was hung up on past versions of myself, looking in the mirror, and saying, "Well, that was the worst software update in the last 31 years of my life," and I kept looking for the uninstall button.

The only way forward to me was backward. I resented my life during that time. All I wanted was to go to sleep and wake up feeling it was all a long nightmare.

We are culturally wired to act up. We are taught wrong concepts of resilience. I grew up to think that it's only through anger, frustration, and control that I can solve my issues and achieve my goals. There was always the black and white, lead or follow, rule or be ruled.

The fact is that there is a vast area in between those two, full of other possibilities, but no one ever tells you about it because it's too chaotic and unpredictable and very different from one person to another.

I identify my rollercoaster of a journey so far into three chapters: The Before, The After, and The Work-in-Progress, through which I found that, however you go, there's always more than meets the eye and that the perceptions and definitions of certain notions like achievements, bravery, failures, self-worth, vulnerability, which I learned growing up, are severely shallow.

My new mantra emerged as a result:

I can rule with love instead of power and surrender with gratitude instead of weakness.

The Bad-ass-ary Bonanza

The before era was what I USED to call the badass version of me, the one who, despite growing up in Lebanon during the war in a broken and dysfunctional family, decided to stand up for myself and make a difference. Somehow, I knew that as a child I may not be able to do much but to grow up. I went to bed every night with nothing to look forward to except that it will be tomorrow, and then the day after, and the day will come when this will all be different.

I figured that the only way I could change my life is to travel. That was my life mission since I was 14, to get the hell out, to live somewhere else seeking a better quality of life and independence. As reasonable as this might sound to many in the conservative community where I came from, especially back then, this was not something a girl would just go out and do. The norm is for a girl to live with her parents until she gets hitched and move to her husband's custody. I grew up challenging every norm, belief, and value system, hustling my way out and willing to do everything it takes.

The dream came true years later when I landed a job in Kuwait as an assistant marketing manager in a big corporation for an international restaurant business. I moved, despite the objections, enjoyed a successful career path, and in a few years, I was head of marketing, running five international brands, traveling the world, and making a good living.

What mattered to me was that I refused to be that girl who was born into shitty circumstances and whose life sucked. I wanted to write my story, to tell the world that what defines who I am is not what I am born into but what I chose to do about it. When I looked in the mirror, that little girl in me would smile.

As great and inspirational as that all sounds, it wasn't the whole story. Little did I know that my strive to hustle and be an overachiever would take a toll on my psyche.

I trust the saying "A clean desk is a sign of a messy drawer." If it looks perfect on the outside, it's rather a turmoil on the inside.

I think we got to a point in this social day and age where it became more imperative to do all it takes to SHOW and PROVE how happy and successful our lives are. I firmly believe that so much of our urge to be better is an interpretation of our need for significance.

We are always struggling and feeling let down as we compare our real lives to someone else's news feed and feel that pressure. There's a pressure to stand out. It is a competition for attention where the stress of answering to expectations is growing. We keep feeling behind because there's always someone out there doing better. So, we try hard to perfect what we have/do/earn/look like, or at least fake it and consequently inflict more insufficiency on others, and the cycle goes on growing into bigger, deeper, and harder snowballs of internal hurdles.

The way I see the news feeds nowadays is like this: strike a pose and write something inspirational completely irrelevant to the picture. Mind you, though, I think inspiration is an amazing quality, and it's great to try to put a positive spin on everything, but the argument here is, what's the real motive? What is more important than being positive is being authentic.

I believe that behind all the empowerment overload there's a deep unintentional avoidance of our messy drawers.

The time came where my drawers were full, and a clean-up was in order.

Anxiety Extravaganza

The after era was an aftermath of an unfortunate withdrawal incident of possibly an overdose, or perhaps a brutal side-effect. Whichever it was, it felt like a withdrawal of my soul from my body, literally.

I was fighting for breath, my heart was pounding faster than I could count the beats, my throat was tight, my head was dizzy, my pupils were dilated to the point I could not see, my hands and feet were numb, my fingers were curled in, and I couldn't force open my palms. The most terrifying feeling was that, during every single minute of it, which lasted for an entire day, I truly believed with each struggling breath that it would be my last.

The after era was post-traumatic stress disorder (PTSD), which, although triggered by the incident, became chronic anxiety and occasional panic attacks, hyperventilating for no apparent reason, pain everywhere in my body, dizziness that was just getting fiercer every time I opened my eyes in the morning. Everything became frightening. It was weird for me to feel that way, and it was hard to admit that those feelings were all the making of my head, based on thoughts about what might go wrong in the future and jumping to conclusions, predicting all sorts of catastrophes that hadn't even happened and likely never would. And although my fears didn't actualize, they sure as hell felt real in my head and in my body.

The worst part wasn't being anxious or feeling the considerable pain; it was the embarrassment. I was ashamed. I didn't understand how that could be happening to me. It was alarming to believe that my inner superwoman had been kryptonited, aka defeated.

I tried many methods to control it. I made all sorts of changes in my life thinking that would help, considered them collateral damage.

Before, I used to do CrossFit and was pretty committed to the whole fitness game, but after I recovered from the incident, I walked into the CrossFit box like nothing had happened, did a long, challenging workout, and finished experiencing shortness of breath and escalated heart beats that just kept increasing long after the workout was done.

That was my very first post-trauma panic attack. From that moment forward, things started to snowball, and I was no longer capable of pushing myself. Mentally I didn't have the stamina. Couldn't handle the hard cardio, as I feared it would simulate a panic attack when I was trying to contain it, so I quit.

My whole self-confidence and pride switched to self-loathing, judgment, and shame. I started looking at myself in the mirror and saying, "Get over it already. You've embarrassed me enough." I was suffering from anxiety and I was unable to accept it. It seemed to me like I was giving myself a restraining order and breaking it time after time.

My lifelong leading by example was falling apart before my eyes. Resentment was all I could feel. I took a hard hit and then followed it by many more; this time, though, I was the one carrying the wired stick, leaving scars with every tap.

My hustle, anger, and go-to frustration mode ran out, and I was compelled into vulnerability. I never imagined that what got me to this point was that I lost connection to my soul, and only through love and gratitude could I reconcile with myself.

Blessings in Disguise

The work-in-progress era was pursuing a different path looking for answers. I embarked on a new journey. I can best describe it as the journey of redefinitions. The one and foremost thing that I could dwell on which I found distinguishing between an imbalanced, stressful, somewhat unsatisfying life and a grounded, peaceful, and joyful one is the connection and depth of engagement we have with ourselves on the one hand and with our belief systems (faith, spirituality or whatever you call it) on the other.

Connection with Ourselves

I started practicing yoga, and when I sat on that yoga mat at first for meditation, I started fidgeting. I couldn't sit still, couldn't silence the voice in my head and couldn't shake off my thoughts. But shortly after, I started learning the power of observation. There's an old Chinese saying: **"If you wish to see the truth, then hold no opinion."**

On the yoga mat, I started to practice leaving my opinion aside and observing my body, my breath, my wandering thoughts, my concerns. I noticed that when I held no opinion, I was more flexible and open-minded. I was capable of feeling compassionate instead of judgmental towards myself. Eventually, I reached out for professional PTSD-specialized therapists and started working on mindfulness.

Connecting to yourself is facing your inner self as an observer, not as the victim or experiencer. Looking at your fears, worries, the cycle of your life…it is reading your story out loud and choosing self-love every time, choosing gratefulness regardless, even during hardships. ESPECIALLY during difficulties.

The Self-Love Mechanisms:

I used to think that every failure was because I wasn't good, talented, or smart enough, and I thought that with this mentality, being my most prominent critic, was my way to strive for improvement.

There's always this image that we look up to that is never ourselves; we are always trying to be that popular person in class, or that smart person in a group, or that pretty person in an outing, or that person I was five years ago, or that person I hope I will be five years from now. But it is never ever the person I am today!

I have this little shit in my head that tells me mean stories, and I guess we all have that. Through mindfulness, I learned that it's nothing but the organ where all the bad memories are stored, the hurt, the shame, the blame, the bullying. I like to refer to it like a computer program, whenever anyone acts seemingly poorly towards you, that memory gets activated, does this chemical connection to whatever is stored there, and generates an emotion, the same feeling of hurt or insult, to which you react accordingly. Frequently, our reactions to situations are nothing but an exhibit of passiveness or self-doubt.

The only way to avoid this mess is if we have enough love and compassion towards ourselves and others. Through practicing a softer approach, I rarely feel attacked or humiliated. Instead, I am capable of seeing the bigger picture, acknowledging the hurtful feeling when it happens, and being mindful of the real source, hence holding space without holding judgment. The softer approach would be seeing ourselves with the set of eyes others see us, obsessing about the things we love about ourselves, not believing our mean little shit when it tells us we are not enough.

I am not saying that we all are the smartest and prettiest and fittest. There's always room to improve our image or nurture our minds or fortify our abilities no matter where we are in life. But hating on ourselves is not the way to do it. Self-motivation through love and compassion will undoubtedly drive better commitment and results.

Practicing mindfulness and self-love broadened my thought process and made me realize that living with anxiety is not weakness; it is actually the opposite. People generally rarely venture outside their comfort zones, but people with anxiety are outside their comfort zones with every single move they make, which is why, through their struggles, they are always stretching their boundaries and consistently winning.

My healing became more focused on letting go of my notions of bravery, expectations, attachments, what I ought to be, and so on, with a long list of shalls and shants, to quit trying and start living, stopped fixing and be PRESENT for what is. Be grateful for every moment of it. Yes, shit will keep falling apart and breaking down, but strength is not preventing or undoing it; rather, it's going through it.

One of the best lines from one of my favorite writers/speakers/human beings, Brene Brown, who specializes in vulnerability and shame studies, reads: **"He or she who has the biggest capacity for discomfort, rises the fastest."**

I got to the point where I started distinguishing between me and my anxiety like they are different entities. My fear has anxieties, I don't, I'd say to myself. It started feeling different. I could sense its existence against mine like two parallel dimensions, and I could deal with it separately. In my head, I could see us both facing each other, sometimes coming into close contact, but no longer mingling as one. So instead of fighting it, I let it flow. I hold on tight, but I hold no judgment.

Connection with Belief Systems

Embracing love was powerful throughout my anxiety-healing journey. However, I still lingered on that trauma and its influence on my life as I know it, and I wished I could take back that one moment.

Practicing gratitude was my biggest challenge, because as much as I found myself in those two years of growing and learning, finding peace and power in acceptance. I was being mindful and opening up to a new world of possibilities I never knew existed. I would still give it all up to go back to the way things used to be, even if that meant going back to complete obliviousness to mental health or to the struggles of the internal demons. I would still rather go back to being egotistical and blindsided, loud and proud, in exchange for never living the pain of that trauma and its aftermath.

One of the biggest fears I developed during my anxiety was fear of the unknown, where the slightest things were magnified into a huge risk in my head. Even when everything seems to be going perfectly well, when I am at my happiest joyous moments, there's this eerie feeling creeping up on me telling me that it's too promising, too good to be happening to me. Before, risks to me were calculated, rational, and obvious; hence they did not get in my way of doing anything that I wanted to do. Big dreams, specific goals, and not much to fear was my equation of winning big. After, however, the risk illusion was around the corner from each step I took. Unknowingly, I started adjusting to my new realities of clinging to certainty and safety with a new equation that went from winning big to losing small.

They say that it is when you feel the least thankful that you are most in need of what gratitude can give you, which was exactly right in my case. I had to find a way to approach appreciation differently. I began cultivating a compassionate approach to embracing everything: the pride of who I believed I'd grown up to be, the pain of my whole experience of post-trauma, the sense of achievement over what I am battling through, and the anticipation of who I keep growing into every minute. My gratefulness started being less of a recreational practice and more of state of mind.

I also started distinguishing between safe, the actual risk, and that wide area in between, and I took steps in that area. A lot seemed to me like a hit and run; however, though, each time, I found myself taking a more significant leap.

With that, I found a new winning small theory. I do not identify failures as such. They are not embarrassments or weaknesses or inadequacies; they are, instead, small wins that I acknowledge and appreciate. Not just because I tried, but also because I seemingly failed, tried again and perhaps failed better, and scored a bigger small win forward.

Here are my top favorite small wins that started small and grew into a bigger vision and path that I am currently walking through:

1- When I acknowledged that I (who always attributed strength to my character) was having anxiety, I won over my preconceived notions and became vulnerable.

2- When I admitted to my friends and circle of acquaintances that I (the woman who everyone knows as a rebel) have PTSD, I won over embarrassment and shame. That actually showed me how much love and support I am surrounded with. I owe so much of my recovery to my friends who embraced my vulnerability and supported me during my rises and falls.

3- I embraced love, I felt connected again, and I owned my story. When I reached out for professional help, I realized that a big part of my anxiety came from my childhood and the deeper issues associated with it—the same childhood I once considered my strength and arsenal that carried me through. Working with a therapist, along with my yoga practice, made me aware that the burden of my struggle with anxiety was weighing me down, and I had to come out of the closet, so I started blogging about it. And the minute I shared that post, I felt ten times lighter.

4- I moved out of my comfort zone. It was hard, and I struggled a lot at first, but I won over my fear and I transformed my life. I came to the realization that I have been stuck in one place way too long, which was Kuwait and my nice corporate job. I was feeling redundant and trapped. Something was missing, and I didn't know what it was, but being connected to my heart and soul helped me see that it was about time to make that move. And that's when Bali called. A couple of my yoga coaches in Kuwait said they wanted to go to Bali. So, I quit my job and the life I'd been living and decided to tag along and embark on this new venture.

I arrived in Bali and reality hit me: I was jobless and away from family and friends; I was so far away from my world of realities—so different from my known habitat. I was waking up every day with no purpose. Not having a place to go, I found myself facing what I was afraid of all along the decision, the change I want to make but wasn't ready for.

In my head, I was giving up every single day, and I was one bad day away from going back. But I knew I didn't go through all the trouble of quitting, moving, leaving the ones I loved, and changing my whole life to go right back into it. I let my heart lead the way. I was happy that I made the move, regardless, and looked for a new purpose.

5- I started doing the things that scared me again. I won over my anxiety. Throughout the search for purpose, a voice in my head that I'd silenced long back was getting stronger: "GET YOUR ASS..." A softer voice interrupted: "Get your sweet ass back into that thing you quit." I walked into a CrossFit box here in Bali, petrified, and I did the very first workout in almost three years after the infamous panic attack! I have been doing high-intensity training for over eight months now, and every time I walk into that place, I win.

6- I was looking for answers, and I found myself. I am a believer that everything happens for a reason, a bigger better idea, but I have avoided facing my trauma from that perspective. I have, until this point, been referring to it as that unfortunate incident and its repercussions. After a few months in Bali, I met a woman who'd had a terrible motorbike accident in Bali. She went through hell, almost died, and suffered so much as a result. At that time, she was at the edge of a breakup with her life partner. During the accident, however, he was by her side day and night and supported her every step of the way until her full recovery. During that time of pain and suffering, they both found peace with each other's company. They found that they belonged to one another, and the whole incident brought them back together stronger than ever. When I asked her how she feels when she looks back at the entire experience, she said she would do it all over again, because it was what got her to a better, happier place with her partner and life.

Her answer hit me! Only then I admitted to myself that seeing the light at the end of the tunnel requires, not only believing in the more prominent reason behind everything that happens but also adopting that belief when my own worst nightmare is what happened.

I'd been trying since then to embrace it, too, to project love and compassion onto that experience of mine and to see the light through the lens of all the beautiful things that I've achieved, which took a trauma, three years of anxiety disorder that shattered me, a complete abandonment of my past life, and letting go of the previous notions of who I am supposed to be and what I held so dear.

As a result, I now realize how going through a near-death experience provoked immense winds of pain and fear. I can see how adjusting my sail through the waves got me to where I am now, and for the first time, I admit that I am eternally grateful for it.

7- When I felt connected again, my attitude towards everything in life changed. I was able to love, trust, and belong.

I didn't come to Bali looking for my own version of Eat, Pray, Love. In fact, I'd never seen the movie before I came to Bali and I didn't make it past India when I tried to read the book, so the whole Bali-equals-magical-love-story didn't resonate with me.

I would be lying, however, if I said that I didn't hope for something different, more profound and real when it comes to relationships. About three weeks into my Bali life, I made one right swipe on my Tinder application, and I met the man I am supposed to be with. What's different about this relationship is that I had to be on a "redefinitions journey" in Bali, not sunk in a hustler work mode, accepting my flaws and becoming the IMPERFECT, connected, grateful version of myself for us to be together.

Reiterating my belief that everything happens for a reason, I have had my share of love and heartbreaks in the past, and I am not an advocate of soulmates. But I know now why every other relationship failure, small or epic, was inevitable. He, together with the updated edition of me, is the reason.

We quickly felt that we were meant to be and wanted to share the rest of our lives together, and we are currently planning our wedding.

8- I wanted to find a purpose; I was inspired into a cause.

In the last few months, given the luxury of time and peace, I connected with different people: women, to be specific, from the Middle East, which is my cultural background. When I shared my stories with them, they were very intrigued to learn more. They wanted to know all about my struggle with anxiety, the transformation, the vulnerability to quit everything and go chasing after a shadow of light. I could see through the sparkle in their eyes how powerful all of this has been. I felt the eagerness in them for a venture into something different.

I got inspired to do something about it. Instead of just sharing stories, I wanted to make a difference, in a way, offer a hand for the women who feel trapped in one place where their social and cultural values do not provide a motivational space for not following the herd—if anything, it actually oppresses it.

For me, this is my way of giving back: to show genuine gratitude towards the awakening journey I am experiencing and the many more to come.

At the moment, I am in the middle of figuring out the mechanism of making it happen. I have my doubts and maybe I'm a little apprehensive. I have never wanted to do my own thing when it comes to work because I was a workaholic, perfectionist, and extremely competitive. But now, recovering from all those traits, I am aspiring to dig deep, all in, savoir-faire, vulnerabilities, insecurities, and workaholism included.

Closing notes

I used to define myself using these words: smart, determined, successful, strong, ambitious. I never thought before how functional and disengaged these descriptions are. In marketing, we call them reasons to buy, and what was missing from that formula are the reasons to believe.

If I defined myself now, I would say: caring, embraced, engaging, influential, inspiring, and—most importantly—grateful. There may have been a wake-up call for me, but I got up, packed up, and went answering although I did not have any plans along the way. I did that because it was time, because I wanted to, and because I looked at myself in the mirror and said, "If it isn't now, then when? And if it isn't you, then who?"

"Whatever you can do or dream you can begin it. Boldness has genius, power, and magic in it." ~ Johann Wolfgang Von Goethe.

"If it's good ~
It's a blessing to be cherished!
If it seems not so good,
it still maybe a blessing in
disguise. Time will reveal.
Be grateful for your blessings
now and those yet to be revealed."

~ Anna Pereira

CHAPTER EIGHT

A Little Story From QZ8501

By Tasha Dietha Amanda

Dream In The Hotel Room

I saw Oscar with his big smile, waving at me. He was far away. I didn't think I could reach him. He was holding his wife's hand then kissed her hand. Suddenly he walked away from her. Moved away and further away until we could not reach him. I could not stop him. He just walked away until I could not see him anymore.

My phone rang, and it woke me up from my sleep. I realized that it was just a dream. But it felt real. I felt exhausted. I was supposed to be at the crisis center, but I didn't feel well. I've gotten my permission not to come in today. The caregivers have hotel facilities for them to stay while volunteering. My phone continued to ring and I tried to find it. Got it. Niya was calling, she's one of my best friends. When I picked up the phone, she took a deep breath before talking. I was teasing her, but she didn't respond. I finally noticed that it might be bad news. I suddenly remembered my dream of Oscar. My heart was beating fast and two seconds later she tried to talk. "We found him, Tasha. They found Oscar's body." She paused and cried while repeating her words.

I didn't know how to react. I was shivering and I felt like crying. But I held back the tears. I was confused because I literally dreamt about him before I got the call. How could this happen? It felt so strange. I wondered what message he's trying to send me. Maybe he wanted to tell me something. I wasn't ready for it. I didn't think I could see him that day. I knew that I should accept the fact that he's dead. His body remains but without a soul. I couldn't believe that this was real. I never thought this could happen in my life. It felt like we just met yesterday, then suddenly he's dead. My best friend Oscar wouldn't be here anymore.

Some of my colleagues came to my hotel room. They weren't ready to go to the crisis center. And we decided to go together. They hugged me as soon as I opened the door. They burst into tears and I felt the same way. We lost a friend and this was something we didn't expect.

I told them about my dream of seeing Oscar. It turns out some of them also experienced the same thing but in a different context. Is it possible that Oscar was trying to communicate with us?

We went to the crisis center room. The crisis center was placed in one of the buildings in the regional police station of Surabaya, Indonesia. The room was filled with people. Full of families who waited on the news, with hopes that they would find their family members. They were families of the passengers of AirAsia flight QZ8501. The accident occurred on 28 December 2014 from Surabaya, Indonesia heading to Singapore. The plane crashed into the Java Sea due to bad weather. 155 passengers died together with seven crew on board. One of the crew on that flight was my close friend Oscar.

With an anxious heart, we entered the building. We met Niya in front of the gate. We hugged and comforted one another by saying, "Everything's going to be okay." We cried together and we didn't realize we created attention from the other families. They approached us asking what had happened and we told them that we found the body of our friend. They felt sorry to hear that. They felt cautious about it because they realized it was going to be their turn soon. After we calmed down, we headed over to the identification room. We were afraid to see Oscar's body cause we couldn't handle it. We discussed whether we should see the body or not. And after a lengthy discussion, we decided not to see it.

Friendship Story

When I joined the AirAsia cabin crew, as a new employee, we needed to attend a training course in Kuala Lumpur, Malaysia for three months. I was having trouble while in Kuala Lumpur because of my English. It was hard for me to communicate and understand the classes. In the first few weeks I had to adapt quickly otherwise I would not be able to pass the test. The Malaysian language helped me a little to communicate because it is similar to my national language of Indonesian.

In the classroom, the teacher spoke in English. The manual books were also written in English. I never understood anything. I even had doubts if I could even pass the exam. There were 15 trainees in my batch consisting of five men and ten women. I was one of the youngest of four girls. Because we were the youngest, sometimes we got special treatment from the other staff.

Oscar and I were doing the training at the same time and his English was fantastic. He always got the highest score in our class. I needed some help with my score if I wanted to pass the exam so I decided to approach Oscar in the hopes that he would teach me. When I asked him whether he would teach me or not, he teased me. Yep, that was Oscar. He liked teasing people, in a good way. Flight attendant trainees must attend the training and pass the exam so that we have the right to fly. The subjects we learned during the training were emergency safety procedures, aircraft introduction, crew resource management, and all the things that are associated with aviation.

After finishing the class, we got back to the apartment building where we were all staying. At night we gather for dinner and sometimes we cooked together. We were doing it every day. At the end of the week, we walk around the city together. Oscar was our leader, so he always arranged our itinerary. He ensured that we were always within reach. He felt that we were his responsibility. He made sure that nothing would happen to us in another country.

Not only that, but he also helped us speak English to communicate with someone we liked. I had an interest in one of the participants from the Philippines. Every time he passed by my class, I tried to communicate with him. But our language was a barrier. I always asked for help from Oscar to translate our conversation. Oscar was still happy to do it cause it was his chance to tease me.

In Kuala Lumpur, I gained a lot of experiences I never had before. I learned English, met new people, explored a new country, lived in a big apartment, partied, barbequed and many more. Sometimes we hung out in Oscar's flat just to cook and have dinner. We didn't realize that we became close friends. We studied together when there was an exam. Oscar always made sure we studied. He would never stop to remind us about studying.

After we had done the exam, we flew back to Jakarta to go through the next step, which was another exam with the government. It made me sad that we were not together anymore. We brought that friendship back to Jakarta, Indonesia when we officially flew as cabin crews.

I was heartbroken one day. I did not leave the room for three days because it was too sad. Every night Oscar will come to my place and knock on my door to invite me over for dinner. He will say things to make me go out of my room. But I still did not leave the room. And Oscar wouldn't give up until I got out. He gave me advice, he made me realize that there is nothing for me to be sad about. But, I didn't want to hear it, even though I knew he was right.

In Jakarta, we always tried to spend time together as we did in Kuala Lumpur. Sometimes we went to karaoke. When we sang at karaoke, there were still people who took over the Mic. Oscar would be one of those people. I would complain every time he started to sing. His was really bad, but he never cared. As much as we protested he would intensify his voice just to make us nag. Whenever we went to karaoke without him, it wasn't as fun. He always knew how to make the atmosphere come alive.

After flying into Jakarta for almost one year. I intended to move to Surabaya. I had one close friend who lived in Surabaya and her name is Niya. She always asked me to move to Surabaya and I finally decided to move and try a new experience. Not long after I moved, Oscar also agreed to move to Surabaya as well. I was thrilled to hear that and some other friends ran as well.

While in Surabaya, I always hung out with them. Just like we did in Kuala Lumpur and Jakarta. I introduced Oscar to Niya and we all become close friends. Not long after that, Niya introduced Oscar to one of her friends. Her Name is Desy. When they met, it was astonishing to us that they got along so well that they ended up dating. I was so happy that he finally found someone. We were often hanging out together. Until one day, I got promoted and moved to Bali.

The Bad News

I was waiting for the announcement to go to the next interview with Emirates Airlines. Becoming a stewardess for Emirates is a dream position of every flight attendant in Indonesia. The destinations that are owned by that company and its advantages are very seductive. Some people who work in regional aviation usually dream to work there. After I passed a few tests, they gave me time to rest while the other group did their analysis.

I checked my phone and I had three missed calls from Niya. I didn't tell her I was in Jakarta to attend the interview. She must be curious where I am right now. She often calls me just to know where I am or she wanted to say she misses me.

I called her back and she answered after ringing three times. "Tasha…" Her voice sounded a little bit worried. "Did you heard about Oscar?"

"No. Why? I didn't hear anything. I'm in Jakarta right now."

"You didn't know? Oscar lost contact." She said.

"Oh, Really? Did he oversleep?" I said without knowing what was going on.

"No, no, no. His flight lost contact with ATC. He flew today to Singapore on flight QZ8501. The flight was supposed to land an hour ago. Flight operation cannot contact the pilot. So they are still trying to figure out what is happening. ATC in Singapore said the plane never landed. It was supposed to be a secret, but it's all over the news." She explained.

I tried to comprehend what was going on but anxiety began to take over. Suddenly, I had no interest with the interview with Emirates cause I was worried. It can't be. Thoughts about the plane crashing popped into my mind. I often heard news about plane crashes, but it's not possible that it would happen to my friends. I prayed that everything would be fine.

After the call, I could not focus on the next test. I didn't think it was the right time so I decided to leave the building. When the news about QZ8501 spread, everyone who knew me, as a flight attendant of Air Asia, panicked and called to ask if I was okay. They thought I was on that flight. I got so many messages and phone calls. I explained to them that I was fine and that I knew the crew on that flight. They were relieved but also grieved that the flight crews were my friends.

My mother panicked when she heard the news. The whole family tried to contact me as soon as they watched the television. When she called me, she was relieved that I picked up the phone. She was glad I was not a victim even though my mother was also sad to hear that Oscar was on that flight. Oscar met my family once. I felt loved and appreciated after talking to my mom. She knew that I was devastated by this news.

I flew back to Bali and heard that the operation didn't get any information from the cockpit. The television was filled with the news about QZ8501. I saw the story about the families who were panicking. They were screaming at the staff at the Airport and I understood their feelings. They were experiencing uncertain circumstances. Was this a mistake or an accident? And no one could give an answer because nobody knows what happened. The uncertainty made people go crazy. We cannot assume that they were in an accident. But people made speculations and it made the situation worst.

I felt I should not be sad even though everyone was speculating. In fact, it is not necessarily true. I thought if you always have negative thoughts, they will materialize. I was too afraid it would happen, and I made myself believe that they were okay. I knew they'd be fine. I made a scenario in my mind about QZ8501 that they landed somewhere. They got into trouble and could not contact ATC. Or they were in a difficult area with no signal. There were many scenarios in my mind, leading to nothing fatal happening to them. It was a relief having thoughts like that. That was how I motivated myself.

I couldn't help but look at the news. All the employees were warned not to watch the news, but I still wanted to know what was happening. I kept turning on and off the television. Not long after that, I saw something on the screen, which made me feel paralyzed for a moment. I saw the photos of the crew who had been on duty for that flight. I knew all of them. I knew the captain who was on duty. He was a great captain. He was a smart and kind person. I often flew with all of them. I couldn't believe that it could happen. My tears welled up and I felt the tightness in my chest. I couldn't help but cry. My heart was torn apart when the search and rescue team found the plane debris. It was heartbreaking. The news confirmed that flight QZ8501 plane had an accident. And the Indonesian people started grieving.

Many Indonesians didn't celebrate New Year's Eve. They all gathered in one place bringing candles and prayed for the victims, this was done in several cities across the country. Seeing that many people, who actually cared, was a beautiful thing to witness. Although it was a sad situation, I knew they got lots of prayers from many people around the world.

After I spent some time grieving and remembering the time I had spent with them. I realized that continued grief was useless. I need to do something to help them and I thought about volunteering as a caregiver in Surabaya. I decided to discuss this with my boss. When I first tried to talk about it, their response was not what I expected. They knew I was close to all of the crew in QZ8501 and they preferred volunteers who are not close to the victims. They were afraid I'd have a nervous breakdown if I became a caregiver. They were worried that I would not be able to deal with the situation. But I didn't give up and kept asking to put me on the list. Every time they looked for the caregiver replacement, I never stopped offering myself. Until they finally gave me the opportunity and tried for a week. I felt glad about that but nervous at the same time. I was glad that I could finally do something. Worried because I didn't know what would happen. I didn't know what the situation would be like at the crisis center.

When I first arrived at the crisis center. I immediately joined the briefing. The team leader gave the caregivers the family names we were going to take care. I replaced one of the caregivers who had to go home because he had been there long enough. Before he left he explained to me about the family, I would look after and he gave me information about that person. The family of the victim I was dealing with was a middle-aged man. After the briefing was over, I immediately searched for the man and tried to approach him. He was very shy and didn't talk much. I introduced myself, but he did not look at me. I asked him what kind of relationship he had with the victim? And the last time he met the victim?

We had a conversation before I took him to see the CCTV recordings before the passenger of QZ8501 boarding. The recording that we saw is a recording of one of the CCTVs that were placed near the security checkpoint before entering the waiting room. This was done to ensure that one of the relatives of the family really was a victim of the Air Asia plane crash. After he watched for some time, he pointed to one of the people on the tape entering a security check and was stuffing his goods into his bag before going through the x-ray. He confirmed that it was his relative. He looked sad. But, he did not want to show it. After he finished, the next family did the same thing. Various reactions obtained as the families watched the tape. It was difficult as they had to watch their relatives board a plane that would crash. I was not strong enough not to cry when I watched their reactions watching the tape.

Oscar's Funeral

After the identification process was complete, Air Asia prepared an Airbus 320 to fly Oscar from Surabaya to Yogyakarta. When we arrived at Juanda Airport, I met many of Oscar's relatives. Before we boarded the plane, an employee in-charge performed a ceremony to move Oscar's body from the ambulance into the airplane. It was quiet for a while. I heard sounds of people crying when they brought the coffin. I saw Oscar's wife Desy from a distance. She didn't look well and she only became worst as she saw his coffin. I couldn't imagine how hard this was for her. This incident must have made her very depressed. They also just got married and Desy was pregnant with his baby. It was unfortunate that Oscar needed to leave this world so fast and wouldn't be able to see his daughter be born.

The coffin was moved into the cargo plane. All the passengers started boarding and I was entrusted to bring the memorial photo of Oscar. I smiled when I looked at his picture. I smiled at his broad smile. He looked handsome in his uniform.

We arrived at Yogyakarta. Then we continued the journey to Klaten. The journey took about an hour by car from Yogyakarta. Many cars provided for the funeral. In Klaten, we did some praying in a mosque before the funeral. In front of the mosque was full of reporters who wanted to capture the moment.

After the prayer was over, they were ready to look at the corpse at the cemetery. We walked along the corpse. As they arrive at the cemetery, they began to move Oscar's body into the grave. It was a sad moment and I needed to say goodbye to him. I should let him go. I knew he didn't want the people around him to feel sad. Being sad wouldn't change anything.

The funeral was finished, some relatives tried to be as close as possible in his grave. Some of our colleagues did the same thing. They've decided to pray while touching his grave and I realized that so many people loved and cared for him. I was glad. I did the same and prayed for him. I touched his grave and shed tears. I said in my heart in the hope that he could hear me, "Thank you for the beautiful moments we shared together. I am happy and proud to have known you. Being your friend was an honor. Goodbye Oscar. We will always love you."

Crisis Center

In the crisis center room, there were many stories. When the families heard the bad news for the first time, they were devastated and cried. But now the families became close to one another together with the caregivers. The crisis center didn't feel like a crisis place, but it felt like a family room where the families gathered, told their complaints and shared their hopes. Sometimes we joked around and laughed with the families. Though sometimes when one of the bodies was found, there was sadness, a sense that they hope it may be one of their families. Some families stayed at the same hotel as the caregivers, so the caregivers also meet with the families at dinner in the hotel.

Sometimes after dinner, some families join the caregivers to chat or participate in singing with a guitar. That is the way we entertained ourselves every day. There are also some families who do not want to get too close to the caregivers. They would keep their distance from us even if one of them got a news update from us. We understood why they didn't want to trust us. But they were nice anyway. There was one family who told about his disagreement with the amount of insurance prepared by Air Asia. They said it's not enough to replace their family member's life. Some families didn't care about the amount of insurance because they feel it's inappropriate to take out insurance from a deceased person.

On the other hand, we as caregivers played an essential role in the crisis center. Each caregiver was authorized to maintain contact with our victim's family. Our duty as caregivers was to make sure that the victims' families are doing well, providing updated information and making sure they got the right information. We accompanied them every day as long as they were in the crisis center. Arranging vehicles for them to come and go back to the crisis center. Sometimes reminding them to eat when it's time. Actually, it's not really part of the caregiver's job but because we spend a lot of time with them cause we feel part of their family. We must empathize with the families of the victims, but we still have to keep the company's good name.

But behind it all, I felt the warmth and the affection in that room, the tenderness from the whole family. I realized how much they loved their family. They were in the crisis center from morning until late evening just to get the update news, "Where is my son's body? My father? My nephew? Or my best friend?" I wondered if the victims knew that so many people were caring for them, they would be pleased. Most people fear that when they die, everyone forgets them and people wouldn't care. But I think they're wrong. This incident made me realize that there will always be people who care. As the caregiver who treats families like their own. I'm sure a lot of people like that are out there. In addition to being close to the families of the victims, caregivers also became close to each other. Caregivers in crisis centers come from different cities. They offer themselves to help the families left behind. I am so grateful to meet and spend time with them. They are incredible cause they sacrificed their work to improve the families of the victims. Although some of them didn't know any of the victims, they still had the desire to help.

After spending time in the crisis center for about three months, I finally had to go back to Bali and continue my work as a flight attendant. The experience gave me a lot of precious memories. I'm glad because at least I could be useful. I've learned so many things from this.

Losing a loved one is not easy. But that is a part of life we cannot avoid. Death sounds bad because we will not see that person forever. But rather than feeling sad when they leave, appreciate the time you've spent with them.

I never thought Oscar would be gone so fast. Several times he tried to arrange meetings for us, but there was always something more important that came up and we didn't catch up. I always thought I could meet him anytime. Unfortunately, there is no other time. Even during his marriage with Desy, he was so mad cause I couldn't make it to his wedding. Although he forgave me, there is a sense of regret that I should have been there. I realized that I should be more appreciative of the time I spend with people around me. Because maybe there will be no other time. Since then I made an effort to take the time to be with the families of the crew, listened to them, and ask how they were doing.

But, if it's too late and one of your loved ones is already gone, live with no regrets. Regrets will not change anything. But learn your lesson and be better. Because there's wisdom behind every incident.

In memory of my best friend Oscar Desano, together with the crew and passengers of Air Asia flight QZ8501.

"Some days
you just have to
create your own
Sunshine"

~ Author Unknown

CHAPTER NINE

Love from Within

By Pendek Sitong

It was a cold, lonely evening. The fireflies seemed to beam their dull lights all over the shadowy jungles laid with dusty road and shade trees in a cocoa plantation in a place called Warangoi in Rabaul in Papua New Guinea. Papua New Guinea is an island north of Australia with a vast land mass and high mountains and rugged terrains, a colony of Australia which gained its independence on 1975 September 16. The villages are usually dark at night with no lights to find your way through. You would bump your feet while you feel your way or allow your pupils to become accustomed to the moonlight or use that light set off by the fireflies. Alone in this Warangoi village plantation, my heart was so darkened with helplessness and despair as I could think of nothing but the emotional pain and sorrow which had been my normal upbringing, but that was my worst night.

I had encountered defeat, a moment in which I couldn't breathe, the shame, the regret, the desire, and the longing of what has happened was only a dream. I thought of all the students in Rabaul High School who had heard the announcement. It was announced as though I was not even there. I felt dirty, filthy, humiliated, and that it didn't even matter I was there. I was made to look as though I loved what I had done and that I was the one who felt so crazy, sexy, and I had raped the little cat down the road. The announcement was made by the headmaster that year, 1985 in December, without mercy or even comfort from him. Fortunately, I had just completed my final examinations.

It was on Saturday that my abusive alcoholic dad had come home and attempted to abuse me with a knife pointed at me. I tried running from him, but he outran me and trapped me, and I fell down and hurt myself badly. He said, "If you run away, I will kill you. Today would be the day you die, and I'll bring you to the morgue if you scream or shout." Fear engulfed me, and I became frozen and couldn't scream or call for help. It was unusual for him to do this to me, and I wondered, why me when I am your child? Tears flowed from my eyes. I knew I would be raped by a monster devil who didn't care that I was his own child. Even my neighbors just watched him as he grabbed my throat forcing me to say my final prayers in my mind. My heart broke into pieces. He forced me to remove my clothes, as he had chased away my mother, who couldn't defend me because of being physically unfit. She had been verbally abused into subjection.

He was attempting to undress me when my mother got my uncle, who came and threatened him, and this upset him. Fortunately, I escaped. The following morning, I went to the police station to seek comfort and revenge only to be demoralized by those who were supposed to help me. They reported the incident to my school, and the headmaster announced the incident at the assembly as if he did justice to himself as he pleased his appetite. The whole student body heard that I was molested by my dad, which was a misreport; however, that was the verdict by the cruel police officer and the headmaster.

My dad was a drunken, abusive man who didn't claim me as his child and had verbally abused me regularly since my mother and I had come to Rabaul in East New Britain Province in 1970. My history was that of shame. My dad said my mum had been pregnant with me before he'd married her, back when she was living in Lae babysitting for her cousin in the late 1960s. My childhood moments were that of hunger and lack of comfort or love from a dad who'd tried to kill me before my fifth birthday. He would drink and come home and beat both my mother and me. It was terror. He would beat me up, hang me upside down, and shut me up in a toilet or a drum and not allow anyone to feed me or comfort me. Anyone who tried to come close to me would be beaten as well. I could go for hours without comfort or food. All I heard said about me was that I was a bastard. I heard him tell my mum to go give me to my biological dad, which she did not understand.

During those years I had three pairs of clothes to cover myself. I would wear the same clothes for years until they tore on me. I remember one such time when I wore the same clothes I'd worn for several weeks to school, and my teacher told me to go home and get changed into better clothes because the school had a visitor. Such was my growing up days in a foreign land. Buying new clothes was thought to be a special blessing, as it happened with much negotiation and hard work on my part, which took four years. Sometimes clothing was donated by other families, as we were originally from Morobe Province and were now living in East New Britain Province, not our home. My mother had three other children, two girls and a boy, despite the ill treatment we received. They, too, were beaten and neglected by our alcoholic dad.

Beatings and hunger were normal parts of our lives. We had to do additional chores to help our parents put food on the table. I felt a great responsibility to take care of my mother and my siblings. I would help with gardening and house chores and took part-time jobs. I dreamed of building a house where I could look after my siblings after every ill treatment I encountered in those years.

The difficulties and pain of having an abusive alcoholic man as a dad was my challenge. I had to collect bottles in the streets of Rabaul to make ends meet. I remember emptying rubbish bins and cleaning the dirt off the bottles in the middle of the night just so I could get breakfast and lunch at school.

One of those nights, my dad came home drunk. He beat my mother and she fainted. I tried fighting back for her. However, he overpowered me, and I went to the police to call for help. The police officers arrived at our house, were told that it was a family problem, and they left. I was beaten badly for reporting to the police, and I fainted. We had neighbors and relatives who tried helping, but they were always beaten by my aggressive dad, and so they watched us suffer helplessly. My father would always pick fights with anyone who tried to help us. He was left to physically and mentally abuse us in a foreign land.

My father worked as a plumber and a driver and would spend all his money on alcohol and gambling. We would go broke borrowing from relatives to pay for food and school fees. I was made to go look for part-time work at a very young age and to do gardening and sell my vegetables for extra cash. Our home was chaos.

I began clinging to Sunday School stories of love and forgiveness taught by German missionaries, and that was comforting for a troubled child such as me. Each time I went to Sunday class I prayed if there was a God to please hear me and save my family.

Most of my weekends were spent with Australian kids who would take me for picnics with their parents. We would go snorkeling and diving and had barbecues on the beaches in Rabaul. I loved those moments; at least I was free from home and the verbal abuse from my cruel dad. A few of the times, they would donate their clothes or buy me clothes as gifts. Then, in the 1980s when we became independent, they left. I was heartbroken, as they were more than friends. I also had other friends from the Chinese community and local people who would help us by donating clothes because we were so poor.

I saw how their mothers drove them to school and came home from work. They would host birthday parties and invite me over. Their mum and dad were loving, and they would treat me kindly as a family friend. I craved their lifestyle, hoping I would someday drive my children to school and celebrate birthdays and donate clothes or food items to the needy. Life for my family was a struggle even then.

Despite our financial constraints, I would come across people with handicaps and I would pity them and give them the last of my coins, even if it was my last, and I would beg my mum to give me at least one coin so that I would give it to them and put a smile on their faces. How I loved to make, them smile. For a small kid with nothing and having the last $20 toea and being able to give it to a handicapped person, leaving me penniless, meant a lot to me.

In school, my siblings and I would not have lunch money to take. We watched other students from well-to-do homes have lunch every day. My mother would wrap my kaukau (sweet potato) in banana leaves, and I would take this to school instead of lunch. I would sneak out and hide somewhere so that no one watched me eat my kaukau, or I just left the lunch in my bilum (traditional stringed bag) and then eat it at the house, or I would throw it away.

The school was exciting for me, as my Australian friends encouraged me by inviting me to their school to watch their quizzes or choir performance and to their fundraising activities at Rabaul International Primary School. They would encourage me to spell words and read little books. I found reading exciting and I started doing well in school during primary school days. I would come in second or third in class. My illiterate parents would scold me and beat me up for making mistakes in school. I was pressured to do better to escape the punishment I received from them. I made it into Rabaul High School in 1983.

During my teen years and high school days, I was banned from socializing or having boyfriends or partying. I would stay at the house and do housework and gardening in the mountains where I could get a clear view of the airport and see the mini jets land and take off. I would dream of sitting in the airplane to go to college. Even then my alcoholic dad continued being violent and aggressive, and his behavior became worse. One of those weekends, my abusive alcoholic dad came home. I was in grade nine when he beat my mother with a rubber hose and almost cut her throat with a knife. My siblings and I ran away into tunnels dug by the Japanese during World War II and slept in there until the early hours of the morning when our cruel dad became sober.

It was there in those war-dug caves, the home of snakes and bats, that I made up my mind that I would do well in school. A bright girl in our school, Helen Mangula, shared with me that she read at least two books a week. Desperate to leave my haunted home, I listened to the nugget she dropped into my life and I read at least two books in a week. My favorite novels were Nancy Drew. Reading in my house was challenging. We only had one lamp, and my family would sit around and tell stories. I would try to get near the lamp to read my books, although I was rebuked for reading books whilst my family had time chatting using the only lamp we had. I would make the decision whether to listen to them or complete my books. The librarian, seeing my interest in going to the library, gave me additional books, and my English teachers gave me extra home work to do, as I was improving and scoring 100% in my English classes. My commerce teacher also saw that I had developed in my commerce class and applied on my behalf to Divine Word University to do accounting when I was still in grade nine. I got accepted. However, my family didn't have the funds to pay for tuition fees that year.

I would burn coconut leaves for light to read or use the moon light. I would not give up; I was determined to do better and leave for a higher institution.

At the end of grade 10 examination, I had a terrible experience, the darkest moment of my life. This was the day that my abusive dad came home drunk pointed a knife at me and attempted to molest me. Attempted incest was normal. I always fought and reported it to my mother, who couldn't do much. I was a child and could do little to defend myself. It all started when I was 15 years old. God graciously helped me out of my father's wicked devices. He had never sexually abused until I had completed my grade 10 in high school.

I felt at least I could use my qualifications to find employment somewhere. I was determined at that time to put an end to my dad's abuse. I was going to yell it out so that the rest of the community would know what a wicked father I had. In that community, they'd always watched helplessly and made fun of us for not living up to their social standards. I was not going to let that man manipulate me anymore. I felt the strength to fight against him. I reported the incident to the police who then made a public announcement to the whole school. The place was no longer a safe community, for the police and the community had over fabricated the story for their interests. I was left alone in a sea of isolation, having no one to ease my pain. That evening, I had nowhere to go. My own home had become a prison, a death compartment. Any moment I could be revenged by my dad. Even the police officers were not helpful. They added demeaning remarks and spread terrible stories. I couldn't get help from them.

I took a bus ride alone to a village called Warangoi to seek consolation from my relatives. I was left scared and rejected, wounded in pain, and the homeless and helpless. No one seems to care. They treated me as though I was at fault. I was abandoned by my mother and friends and relatives. I was sore to the bones and sick in the heart. I lost my appetite and did not eat for one week. Dirty with no clothes, no money, and afraid my dad would come looking for me to end my life, I was a mess. I lost all hope, and despair swallowed me up. My future was grim. I lost the respect of everyone and all my friends left me. I felt alone. So alone, covered in a blanket which never brought warmth, only regret.

It was a cold, lonely evening. After much thought, the moment when I had had enough of the pain that was piercing my spirit, I walked toward the cliff knowing that I would end the shame by jumping off or hanging myself on a rope. Something compelled me to stop. It was as if I heard the voice right inside me saying, "Why are you doing this to yourself? Where are you going after you end your life? You'll end up in hell." The voice startled me, saying, "I'll never leave you nor forsake you." It was as if someone stood right behind me and said that. "I will be your friend until the end of your life on earth."

In January the following year, 1987, I was accepted into Aiyura National High School. I was one of the top five students that year, and I was accepted on full scholarship with airfares and tuition fees to continue my studies. I left that year with donations from kindhearted relatives who gave clothes and funds for me to pay for necessities. After all the pain I'd suffered, I left excited to continue my education despite all the pain and harassment and negative circumstances. I wanted to be educated at a university or college. My goals were slowly happening.

How I loved to move away from my family and the ill treatment and mostly my alcoholic dad. I met many wonderful and loving people who were my teachers. Mr. and Mrs. Lero Maka were very special to me. They had three children and were both from the Highlands of Papua New Guinea. The rumors I'd heard about Highlanders were very negative. I didn't know different until I met them. They took me into their home as parents and away from my own troubled home. Never did I know there was such a home filled with love and respect for each other as husband and wife. They showed a lot of love and respect for me and the other students who came to their home. I had a lot of appreciation for the Highlanders because of them. This couple had a special kind of bonding between them. It was love. The husband was soft-spoken and addressed his wife and the other women with a lot of consideration.

Anna Kila, a New Zealander, was another one of those kind-hearted people. She was my class patron who would prepare my favorite food and tuck me into bed and kiss me goodnight. She was loving and chose not to marry until her old age in Papua New Guinea. She had love for her students, and most students speak highly of her even to this day.

Most of all, in 1986, I met Christ and made Him my Lord and Savior. He is the pillar that made me succeed in life. I literally said yes to love, light, and forgiveness. I learnt God was triune. He was the creator of the universe who gave His Son to die for me, the wicked sinner. I found love and light and forgiveness and newness and the ability to forgive myself and others who had sinned against me. I found the ability to live life in spite of its challenges.

Life in school away from home was challenging. I met good people who loved the hurt away from me. They provided parental advice. I was comforted and never bothered having a boyfriend. I concentrated on completing my education even though boys wanted to date me. I participated in Christian religious activities. During that year, I was free from the trouble back at home. I took all the time to enjoy being away from an alcoholic dad. I was free at last. I loved my space so much. I had total freedom. I enjoyed the climate and the people and forgot to concentrate on my studies. I had planned to graduate and go into university to study law. However, I didn't make it, and I went to Divine Word University to take up Allied Health Sciences and studied Health Officers Studies, a course that is the equivalent of Rural Medical Doctors.

In 1988, I remained at Divine Word University and continued the training for three years. At the school, boys were allowed to enter into girl's rooms and vice versa during our second year. We all shared the same dormitory. A few of our girls lost sight and got pregnant, and some of our boys got expelled from school.

I was selective of the boys who asked to date me. I never wanted anyone who was a drunkard or chewed betel nut or smoked. That year in college, I met a handsome young man who stole my heart even before I knew what he was really like. He was neat and tidy, had white teeth, and had never smoked or chewed betel nut. He was loving and kind. He said all the nice words and did all the loving deeds a girl would expect from a boyfriend, and I fell in love with him. He was my first steady boyfriend. I had limits in relationships, and he respected that he was only allowed to hold hands with me. His name was Mima Wakimsep, a young man from Telefomin who trained in the same profession as me. We promised each other that nothing would happen until we both completed our diplomas, and we supported each other to achieve this goal. He graduated first and was working before me. I continued for another two years and graduated with a diploma in the same course.

I felt that I had achieved my dreams on the day I graduated that year. I sighed with relief and was ready to be employed with a health extension. As the only girl in my family and clan to have come this far, my people were proud that I was determined to finish. I felt joy for the achievement and could see the respect from my former high school and college friends. Even my own family was proud of the achievement.

Getting employment was challenging, as most graduates had their own choice of where they would be employed. I wrote to different government entities and was offered employment in three different locations. I chose to work in Morobe Province. I was offered a position in one of the most remote areas, and I took the challenge as a young rural assistant medical officer, knowing that few people wanted to be posted there. I remain an employee of the department of Morobe until now. I have encountered a lot of challenges, being one of the three female District Health Manageresses in a profession highly dominated by men. There is a total of nine District Health Manager positions, and six are occupied by men. Work has been challenging. I have encountered a lot of discrimination and sexual harassment in my work place. In Papua New Guinea, males look down on females. However, I took the initiative to be proactive in my profession and worked my way up to the middle management level.

I married Mima Wakimsep, my first college boyfriend. We were friends for over three years, just holding hands during our relationship. It took him three years of courting and then he proposed to me on our graduation day. We were both in our mid-20s when we married. I introduced him to my family and he asked them to allow him to marry me. Our families agreed to the marriage. In 1992, we had a legal marriage and then had two lovely children. Emmanuel Wakimsep, the eldest who is now 25 years old, and Deborah Wakimsep, who is 20. My husband was everything a woman could long for. He would help with the household chores. He would bring his paycheck home, and we'd do our budget together with the pay we both brought home. My husband never drank alcohol or smoked cigarettes. He was such a lovely person. However, he had a weakness in chasing different women.

His indiscretion totally changed me into a jealous, bitter, angry, unforgiving person. My attitude toward him pushed him away. He refused to come home to the children and me for longer periods, and then he would return and seek forgiveness from the three of us when he was broke or got sacked from employment. I found him with several different women who were younger than himself and me. I resented him as my husband, and I insisted that he leave our house. Quarreling about small things was normal. The gap between us slowly widened, and my husband left me for several different women since 1998, making me and the kids suffer.

Finding out my husband was womanizing was a low blow for the children and me. I would go for days without the desire to eat. I would pray to God to heal my marriage and bring my husband back.

I questioned a lot whether or not my prayers did work or if there was a God who would listen and heal my life and my marriage. My husband continued to fool around with so many women that I had to forgive him more than 10 times until I decided to cut off the cycle and move on without him. This happened until I changed my perception. I chose to forgive him and the women who were offending me.

Until I found that I was the problem and my impression was wrong, I couldn't win. I was sick and lonely and had two children to raise alone. The prayers that I articulated formed the results of what I needed. I needed a miracle, and it happened that I saw God intervene in a miraculous way. It seemed so different.

I was praying using the name of Jesus over a patient who had a swollen abdomen because of an enlarged liver, and spleen. As I put my hands over the spleen and the liver, they just fell into their standard sizes within seconds. This happened twice. I was entering into something I couldn't explain and can't tell now, but this was happening at the mention of the name of Jesus.

I asked for a vehicle and a decent job, and I was given them. I had special visitation by angels who visited for one month and pointed us to specific locations where cursed objects and ginger were buried on our current property. These were discovered and disposed of in the river.

I learnt to be open to the truth and to take possession of who I really was inside.

The jealousy, the anger and bitterness, the hatred, and the demanding nature and the selfish person I was became apparent to me. I found out I was critical and abusive in the usage of words. I had poor perception of my physical image, a poor self-image. I thought I was the most righteous person on earth and verbally abused others whilst I was hurting and hiding my past realities.

Being a single mum, I feared my children not getting a proper education, so I had to work hard to put my children into international schools in which they did well, scoring straight A's. After the necessary education, they were both transferred into our public school system, and they both did well. I sent my son to Aviation Australia, and my daughter went to a business college in our country and graduated with a diploma. My son is currently employed with Summer Institute Linguistics, whilst my daughter has applied for employment and is awaiting their response. Both my children are very bright. Competing with international students and scoring straight A's was such an achievement for them. They could have done much better; however, their father was regularly flirting with women, and it disturbed their performance in public schools, and the students in there were continually fighting, disrupting the students' performance. It was difficult for many parents, and many students dropped out. Very few made it to university and colleges as my children did.

My biggest challenge came when my ex-husband went to prison. I was battling the rage of hatred towards him. I had to face the reality of him having no friends, and of having said my vows some 26 years earlier. He was cunning since he had no friends, not that I wanted us to be reunited as a couple, but I wanted to forgive him and do good to him and to free myself from the prison of hate.

Well, I am so free now and looking forward to doing other projects with the handicapped and also to helping women who are homeless and living in the streets in Lae. I have been part of groups that bring food and clothing to people living on the streets in our notorious sex-trading sites in our city. We have worked with women trying to rehabilitate them and hoped to get them out of the sex industry. We have used our own homes to bring them and have nursed two women who had HIV to rehabilitate women in our community. Doing this kind of activity is challenging. You get branded for hanging with such a class of people.

I was running from the truth until I realized I was only hurting myself. I chose to love me, to forgive, to face who I really was, to love the person I was seeing in the mirror. Change is slowly coming my way.

I continue to read books on personal development and the Law of Attraction, books by writers like Napoleon Hill and Dave Ramsey, and I've watched The Secret and other encouraging films. I am walking on a journey which people are gracing. I am a Christian. I read the Bible, which talks about God's love through Jesus Christ. These all point to the one message: to get me together within and walk and talk the life within.

Fortunately, I picked up the book Barefoot Investor and Dave Ramsey's Total Money Makeover and Robert Kiyosaki's Rich Dad, Poor Dad, and I am preparing to retire at 50. I consider myself an average mum who is determined to reach my life goals, which includes starting up a business and buying a proper house, working on my handicapped project, and delivering women out of the sex trade.

I look forward to engaging with individuals and attending seminars that will enable me to achieve my goals. I love reading and using the internet to listen to other people's success stories.

"Your greatest test
is when you are able
to bless someone else
while you are going
through your own storm"

~ Regina Malabago

CHAPTER TEN

OVER AND BEYOND TRAUMA

By Eui J Jung

In April 2018, in my dream state, I heard a voice telling me to "Find Keala." Surprised by the clear voice, I woke up and found my sleeping wife next to me snoring. I searched the internet for "Keala," and found "Keala Settle – This is Me. The Graham Norton Show. 9 Feb 2018" in YouTube. Keala said that she was successfully hiding for 25 years in New York City, and it was Hugh Jackman's fault. I had no idea what that meant.

A month later on a sunny bright clear Saturday morning, I attended a Toastmasters club as this is my routine on weekends. I saw a guest from Indonesia with an Australian accent, John Spender. And this chance meeting resulted in me writing this chapter after 25 years of military service in the Korean navy. No more hiding. And it is John's fault?!

I was born 21 years after the Operation Chromite (Battle of Inchon) during the Korean War. My grandfather once told me that he brought his family from North Korea down to South in winter in pursuit of freedom at the time of Chinese intervention. He left everything behind, even his own parents and siblings in the north of 38th parallel. He had to start all over by himself to support his family as a carpenter. I learned the Korean and Chinese characters and letters from him. He was a knowledgeable and wise old gentleman.

On the contrary, my father is an alcoholic and has dementia, and is in a sanatorium. This is how I grew up. My mother sometimes told that she could not breastfeed me when I was a baby because she was not able to produce milk for a newly born baby even after 10 months of pregnancy. My sister was born one year after me. As my sister and I grew up, I was often told by my parents to yield my possessions to her because she is younger than me. I didn't have many happy memories with my family members in Inchon.

Now I'm a husband to a lady and a father to a girl. A daughter of my father's friend became my wife, and we have a daughter. I persuaded my wife that we should enjoy traveling as often as possible to make happy memories together, which was successful for the past 15 years.

When I look back on my experiences in this life, no way return or no detour would be the best description of them. When asked about what 'Love and Gratitude' may mean to me, I would refer to them as energy and everything positively and productively. So, in this context, I would like to begin by applying to myself as an observer of the physical reality as a Particle in Event Horizon. Now, before going further, I want you to enjoy the wild experiences I have gone through. Don't take it seriously. Sit back, relax, and look into it.

One summer day, at the age of 13, I went out to swim with my uncle and cousins at a beach in Busan, Korea. While enjoying swimming and riding tidal waves not far from the beach, I failed to escape from a mass of powerful swell that overridden me. I was pushed down by the enormous force of sea water and rolled into the deep. I struggled to catch a sip of air above the surface. Then I exhaled the last air bubble through my mouth. And with a taste of salt water, the water poured through every opening of my body. A heavy smash on the back of my head knocked me out.

Instead of being dull and dizzy, my senses became vivid and clear. Under the sea, the above calm bright light was shining so warm and soft, which at the time was perceived to be the sunlight being splashed as the surface waves. The feeling I encountered was so comfortable, nice, wonderful, and cozy that I felt I'm home. I began to follow the source of light - bright but not hot; joy, happiness, and tranquility; and "unconditional pure Love" were the precise keywords and right description for it.

A magnitude of attachment to the back of the light drew my attention like an anchor and chain and made me look back. Surprisingly my physical body was there, and at that moment I was soaked up to it. My eyes popped open, and I thought to myself: "How long have I stayed under the sea? Whatever that light was, I need to go up and catch a breath." My body was so heavy that I could not swim upward; instead, I was dragged down to the bottom. Upon touching the bottom, I had to crawl like a crocodile upslope to the beach. After I beached out, it was painful replacing the seawater in the lungs into the air that we normally breathe: Ihad to vomit the sea water in my lungs through my mouth, nose, and even eyes. It might have been tears, though. Strangely, I felt the density of my body in the sea was rather relaxing and stable than above the surface.

Around the age of 16, while having lunch with my father, he suddenly smashed the table with his chopsticks, and said that he didn't receive any heritage from his father, not even the chopsticks; and such would be the case for me too. I lost my appetite of having a meal with him ever since that happened. My mother once told me that I had to find a scholarship for my higher education because they can't afford it. It felt like I was left alone and abandoned. I thought to myself that it was time for me to leave my parents and to be independent. At the age of 17 to 19, during my high school days, I did well on exams, proving that I was ready for the next step, which was to go into higher education. My solution was to study even harder for an exam to enter a university.

In the late winter at the age of 19, my failure to enter the Korean Air Force Academy in pursuit of free education led me to think of jumping off from a building - suicide. I found myself standing up on top of the Memorial Hall for Inchon Landing Operation. One step forward would be an end of the story. Before doing that, just for the last moment I looked around, felt the wind touching my cheeks, saw the blue sky, took a deep breath and heard a bell. Bell? Yes, a deep sound of a bell.

Suddenly, I became curious about what it was. It felt like waves of magnetic forces pulling and withdrawing me. I decided to hold my suicide to find the source and went in the direction where the sound was coming from. I found myself standing in front of an old Korean style building. I saw strange statues, figures, and atmosphere not knowing what those were, and was attracted to one of the pillars with five Chinese letters. It roughly translated into "Everything is made by Heart." Even though I had the knowledge of each letter, an idea of 'I don't know' struck me bad enough to forget what I was doing. I stood there a couple of hours appreciating and comprehending its meaning. The five Chinese letters imprinted in my brain and mind followed by questioning 'What's that?' It's still with me always asking the same old question. But it comes up with fresh new answers every time. Saved by the bell? Yes!

One year later I pass the exams to enter the Korean Naval Academy for free education. And my life away from my parents successfully made its way. The benefit of free costs me four years of military training and five years of mandatory service as a navy officer. Marrying my wife made me reconsider retirement, so I continued my journey with the navy and defense.

At the age of 27, I was a junior navy line officer. After completing three months of cruise training on the sea for midshipmen of the Naval Academy, I was rewarded a week of vacation. I bought a 125cc motorbike, drove up to Inchon from Jinhae for two days. Spent a couple of days with my parents and high school friends, then I headed back to our ship. In Jochiwon, on my way back from Inchon to Jinhae, I got into an accident. At a downhill, I stepped on the accelerator and gained speed. At the end of the road, it was curving steeply to the right. Because of the high speed, taking a turn in my lane was not possible. Seeing the yellow line and tires of an oncoming car on the opposite side of the road, instantly I knew I was going to die under that car, and made a decision to die anyway just by crashing against the car upfront straightforward. There went a clean "Boom." I remember that I had an impact on my left knee and then knocked down on the ground. In between those two, what happened?

It was wonderful. No words can describe the instant while my body was thrown out off the bike, impacting against the windshield of a car, flown over the roof, and watching my body as its happening. It was like I was accompanying my body, in slow motion, flying in parallel. It was fantastic. No fear, just "unconditional boundless Love."

Got back to my body and collected the broken pieces of my knee bones. Got in an ambulance, headed to the hospital for treatment, and I had a couple of operations. I saw my open wounds and touched the bones of my body. It was beautifully white and had no touching senses there. Instead, the pain was merely on the skin and muscles. I have to befriend pain, as it will accompany me throughout the rest of my life.

In November 2007 until 2008, I joined a UN mission in Sudan (UNMIS) to Africa for Peace Keeping Operations (PKO) as a Military Observer (MilObs). Personally, it was like heading to the unknown world of fires: a little nervous, and a lot curious; and it's a mission!

My idea of being a member of the armed force is that it is a unique "privilege" to go to war or somewhere under armed conflicts. It's not fighting for something more or else, but for defending those who you love, even though it's uncertain whether you are coming back dead or alive. My application to deploy to the navy 2nd fleet, which is located in the west of the Korean peninsula, were all rejected. There were two Battles of Yeonpyeong in 1999 and 2002, and also ROKS Cheon-an sinking in 2010 there. The rejection made me look for something else beyond the navy. An opportunity came from a different warring zone in Africa, which situation on the map seemingly more or less looked like that of Korea. Had an interview with General Officers at Joint Chief of Staff (JCS), got several vaccines injected, received a one-way ticket from UN Department of PKO (DPKO), my bags were packed, tears ran on my wife and daughter's eyes, no promise that I would come back alive. Boarded a plane at the Incheon international airport, it took off and landed. Boom, there I was in Khartoum, Sudan, Africa. It was in November, which was the winter season in Korea. But it was the dry, hot season in Sudan. My first impression there was the heat choking my throat and taking my first breath. I was overwhelmed by fear of what would happen during my tenure of duty for one year. I wished that nothing bad would happen to me. However, it proved to be an expectation.

My duty station was notorious for being the most horrifying and dangerous team-site ever amongst all the other sites in the Mission, Abyei, the sector with only one team-site. Mostly a sector has 4~5 team-sites. The situation there in Abyei was historically so intense that armed conflicts were occurring almost every other week. I blame nobody for posting a navy officer to a desert area. The UN headquarters might have a reason for that, which I couldn't comprehend. Otherwise, my life has the reason.

In March 2008, I was a patrol leader of stand-by UN Military Observer (UNMO) team. All of a sudden, I was called and tasked to launch a patrol north of the town to investigate an armed conflict. The information was that the two conflicting parties, one was a military force and the other was a civilian and that UN Police (UNPOL) would launch their patrol as my team was heading for the scene. On my way to the scene, we encountered a group of pickup trucks. We stopped them to ask questions, I saw a man lying in the back of a truck. They were carrying a dead body. I asked them what happened to him. They said that he was dead because of a car accident between two vehicles: one was a military-heavy truck, and the other a mini-van. It was confirmed that the body wasn't bleeding out, which simply meant that he didn't get shot nor fractured out. Instead, several swollen parts showed that the cause of his death was severe internal bleeding. I touched the dead, so I could check his body temperature and confirmed that he died not long ago. And I saw his face. It showed that he didn't die suffering slowly. He looked like he finally found peace. However, it was not even close to a good sense - touching an unknown dead body.

In May 2008, the conflicting parties were severe. The situation escalated, and UN civilian staffs evacuated. Only UNMOs and military members were allowed to stay in the UN base. Then there was a fight in the middle of the night under the moon. Soldiers were shooting guns, launching rockets, and tanks were firing. And the UN base was in-between the fighting forces. They were using it as their shelter. Bullets and rockets fell into the base causing damages.

Luckily I was not there. I was on my way back to Abyei from Khartoum from my leave. Brazilian, Canadian UNMO colleagues and I had to stay overnight in the Kadugli sector, where there is an airport to change flights from a one-aisle passenger plane to a helicopter. We were allowed to redeploy to our duty station a day after the clash. As we were closer to the helicopter landing pad in the base, we could witness that almost everything in the surroundings of the UN base was burnt down to ashes.

In June 2008, a group of US politicians paid a visit to Abyei sector to monitor what was going on there on the ground. UNMOs were tasked to take the wheel to escort them out of the base. We had to see, smell, hear and touch the battleground. It was not a movie set or virtual reality. Our security and safety could have been under threat and in danger at any time while we were on patrol. Dead bodies were everywhere and it smelled awful. After that, UNMOs were tasked to launch more patrols to the town and made reports to UNHQ in Khartoum. We launched many foot patrols and walked corner to corner. The dead bodies soon became skeletons and somehow, dogs got fat.

Humanitarian aides and local habitats slowly came back, cleaned the mess to rehabilitate, and gradually restored the town. There's a saying that the pen is mightier than the sword. In my observation, it was on the contrary. I would say that the gun is faster and mightier than the paper.

In July 2008, a team of UNMO patrol was launched to the south of Abyei with a group of five members in two vehicles. In the first vehicle were a UNMO from Philippines (Patrol Leader) and me (Driver) and in the second one a UNMO from Benin (Driver) and two National Monitors from each conflicting parties. This was not the recommended composition of a patrol team, but the three gentlemen from Africa wanted to share a vehicle.

The patrol successfully performed the verification of an armed force and the monitor of their movement. And we decided to conduct the UN presence to the local marketplace in Agok. Even though I was not comfortable or convinced, I had to be with the team. It was like I'm heading for the graveyard with the group.

Local people there in the marketplace soon recognized one of the team members who was a National Monitor representing their enemy. A fistfight began because UN PKO doesn't allow us to be armed for the peacekeeping job, and also the raged local civilians didn't have firearms either. It was time to withdraw our presence there. We didn't run so as not to gain unnecessary attention from others, but it was in vain. I led my team back to the vehicles in a parking area. To open the door, I turned around and looked back, and was surprised to see many people were after us. They were saying that the UN brought a spy. Five members got back in each vehicle and locked the doors. The local people gathered more and more and surrounded the two UN vehicles. They shook the vehicles, tried to open the doors, smashed the windows, and yelled at us.

The vehicles were ignited, engines running, and about to move. Suddenly a soldier appeared, and he was shooting at the 2nd vehicle in which the National Monitor was. I witnessed everything as it happened. The team members in the vehicle got shot and blood was spilling inside. It was like watching "bloody red" popcorns popping in the oven. Instantly I knew I would be the next victim. At that moment, I got white-out and sensed an injection on my head pushing flashback memories with my wife and daughter in Korea. It gave me a reason to live and survive to see them again. What options did I have? I thought about killing the shooter by running him over using our vehicle. It's an impulsive thought fueled by anxiety and anger. Suddenly, a gentleman in a white jalaba showed up and calmed the soldier. That was the only chance to escape the scene in compliance with the UN Rules of Engagement (ROE). One was bleeding on the head, and the other on the shoulder. No more victims.

On the radio, I requested a Medical Evacuation (MedVac). A helicopter was on standby to take the wounded to a high-level hospital. As soon as the injured boarded the helicopter, it took off from the land with a thrust of dust. Watching it fade away into the sky, tears filled my eyes with the emotion of sorrow, and a sense of guilt and responsibility. What if I had insisted on not going to the marketplace? Had it not happen? And had been a different story?

In Nov 2008, my tenure of duty in the mission came to an end and I returned to where I started the journey a year before. The perspectives and senses of reality changed from those of before. Every night a repetitive nightmare suppressed me: in the dark, shadows surrounded me, fought back, and doomed with a nice clean shot from a sniper. And then I woke up with cold sweat all over my body, sometimes yelling and mourning. My wife told me that I move too much that she could not sleep next to me. We didn't understand what I was going through. I've consulted a psychologist in military hospitals, but nobody knew, and maybe nobody cared.

In March 2010, ROKS Cheon-an sinking happened, and ROK Navy lost lives of sailors. In 2012, I had a chance to work with the Commanding Officer of the ship in the Naval Education and Training Command in Jinhae. One day we were drinking beer talking about what we have gone through in the past. Suddenly he was pointing at me saying that I had trauma, which was the first time that I recognized I was crying. Why was I crying?

I didn't know the definition of trauma. Wikipedia was the first resort to define it. Between him and me, it was like a man knows a man; the patient knows the patient; however, doctors didn't see the pain in patients, but know the malfunction of candidates.

I learned Vipassana meditation from a Buddhist monk in Busan when I was in my early 20s, and practiced more after realizing something was wrong with me. Breathing in and breathing out rise and fall, observing the five senses of the body, strolling sensing from the feet, etc. gave me a space to look over and into what is going on with my memories, thoughts, and emotions. It's like watching a periscope in a submarine. It's an exercise observing the physical reality within the physicality with at least 3rd person's point of view.

Since the mid-30s, Chen Taichi came to my attention. Also after realizing something mentally wrong with me, I densely practiced it. It may seem a kind of "slow dance," but is a form of martial arts that is famous in China. It is a powerful way to observe the flow of my intent, the movement of my body, and the flow of heat or energy. And it should be slow enough to catch all the above mentioned three in one.

I joined a Toastmasters club in Seoul in my late 30s, several times attempted to quit and disappear, but still cannot avoid the temptations of making stories out of the experiences I've gone through. Every time I organize a story, it gives me a chance to look back on the experiences and memories as a 3rd person composing it. In the mid-40s, I made a decision to keep moving on with Toastmasters.

The process of making stories and presentations from the experiences is like washing dishes after a good dinner. I should experience it first and then tell a story. Taking roles in a meeting, taking the responsibility of a club officer, and taking an obligation of the mentor in a club are not just nonprofit services to other members. But rather the benefits are to those who perform them, which is rewarding to become a better me. It also first gives me experiences and then chances to heal myself by myself.

Something has changed. In the nightmare which was doomed with no escape at the end, I was flying with electric lights in the Heart area and magnetic fields around me. In that dream, I was a ball or orb of electricity and magnetic, giving light to the shadow beings, and then joining back to a city of light. Yes, it was the city of light.

Like it or not, my definition of life is a collection of experiences within the scope of five senses can reach, which may be termed as the physical reality. Studying death gave me an idea that there's something else beyond it. It may be returning to where I belong or moving to another dimension. I'm not praising the death, instead of trying to look through and beyond it. No reason not to explore it. What I know now is that I love my life as a human being and appreciate the experiences during the course.

To this day I'm still questioning the meaning of imprinted letters, 'Everything is made by Heart.' This question drove me to the 'I don't know' state and made me question everything that comes to my attention even though I don't have a concrete answer to it. Amongst which, megalithic structures, Sanskrit civilization, and the Universe are those in my area of interest. My understanding of them may be different from the mainstream, but I like it.

Here's my own interpretation of Love and Gratitude: Love is energy, and Gratitude is gravity. It's worth living on this planet with them, cause without them, we don't exist.

"The way we chose to
see the world creates
the world we see."

~ Barry Neil Kaufman

Author Biographies

John Spender

Chapter One

John Spender didn't learn how to read and write at a basic level until he was ten years old. He has since traveled the world, started many businesses, leading him to create the award-winning book series A Journey Of Riches, he is an Award Winning International Speaker and Movie Maker.

John was an international NLP trainer and has coached thousands of people from various backgrounds through all sorts of challenges. From the borderline homeless to very wealthy individuals, he has helped many people to get in touch with their truth to create a life on their terms.

John's search for answers to living a fulfilling life has taken him to work with Native American Indians in the Hills of San Diego, the forests of Madagascar, swimming with humpback whales in Tonga, exploring the Okavango Delta of Botswana and the Great Wall of China. He's traveled from Chile to Slovakia, Hungary to the Solomon Islands, the mountains of Italy and the streets of Mexico.

Everywhere his journey has taken him; John has discovered hunger among people to find a new way to live, with a yearning for freedom.

He also co-wrote the script for the film Adversity and interviewed all the guests, including Jack Canfield, Lisa Garr, Dr. John DeMartini and Dr. Micheal Beckwith to name a few.

For more information about contributing to the A Journey Of Riches series contact John.

Email; jrspender7@gmail.com.

Facebook: https://web.facebook.com/john.ajourneytoriches

Marina Pearson

CHAPTER TWO

Marina is a Mama, Bestselling author, Investor, Joy of Being Podcast Host and Joyriding Retreat Facilitator. Aside from being on ITV This Morning, Marie Claire, The Guardian and The Daily Mail she lives her life working on projects that light her up.

When she isn't spending time with her son at the beach in Javea, Spain (where she lives) she is running exclusive Joyriding Retreats in Spain for women/mums in business who want to ditch the overwhelm or overseeing her investments, she hosts her Joy of Being Podcast where she interviews transformation professionals, business owners and creatives on how to live a life and business that they can really enjoy.

If you fancy finding out where your joy gaps are and what you can do about them do so here www.marinapearson.com/scorecard

Instagram:@marinapearson

Facebook: Marina C Pearson

Podcast: http://bit.ly/JOBP2018

Gretchen Phillips-Williams

CHAPTER THREE

First, and foremost, are Gretchen's roles as a mother, fiancée, sister, daughter, and friend. She always strives to put her family and friends first, while not forgetting to care for herself. She juggles all the family activities on top of working full-time as the Assistant Director of Admissions for a law school.

It took nearly 20 years in Corporate America before Gretchen finally took a chance! She became involved with a multi-level marketing company. The company was not right for her, but it forced her to venture out of her comfort zone, and she met some amazing people. This experience and these people are what started her on her development journey. In turn, this allowed Gretchen to realize her passion for helping others.

She now uses her years of marketing experience, technical skills, and extensive business knowledge to assist others in her community that are looking to start a new business or take their current company to the next level. She loves seeing the positive, ripple effect this has on the local community and all its members. Gretchen is also very passionate about personal development. She desires to help empower others to realize the magnitude of their full potential.

Cheryl Maria Marella

Chapter Four

Cheryl Marella is a TV and Radio Personality in Indonesia. She started her media and journalism career as a radio DJ at MTV on Sky radio in 2003, and MTV VJ Hunt 2007 finalist. From there, she hosted shows in media companies such as 101 Jak FM, Discovery Turbo, MTV Indonesia, CNN Indonesia, Channel News Asia and was featured on The Source TV – Fullscreen Media.

She is also an M.C., Moderator, Public Speaking Coach and Digital Marketer. Her passion is to empower, educate and inspire women around the world to love themselves, and to awaken as many people as possible of the importance of their self-improvement. She is now working towards her dreams of having her own company and animal ranch to create a home for abandoned and neglected animals in Bali.

Leanne Cordova

Chapter Five

Leanne Cordova is a qualified NLP and Hypnosis Coach who uses her education to help others navigate their life paths. Leanne was initially drawn to this industry when she found herself leaving a toxic relationship while being pregnant and caring for her young son.

From here it sparked her desire for continual learning and development and has led her to spend the last five years volunteering her services and training under some well-known personal development speakers.

Leanne has been building her following and has created a space online where she mentors others interested in creating the financial lifestyle they desire using and implementing the techniques she has learned.

She is an avid believer in preventing dis-ease in the body and has spent the last two years developing a higher understanding of how to nourish her body through healthy eating, movement, and meditating incorporating the mantra of 'How can things be better than this' throughout her daily life.

Connect with me and follow my journey online and remember to embrace love and practice gratitude every day.

https://www.facebook.com/LifeBuildingDreams/

https://www.facebook.com/public/Leanne-Cordova

Fernanda Lorenti

CHAPTER SIX

Fernanda Lorenti is an international transformational speaker, coach, and actress.

Today, in addition to being a mom, a working Hollywood actress, and model, Fernanda is a personal and business mentor, a transformational and leadership speaker.

She is the driving force behind the personal development and leadership seminars she conducts in the US and Brazil, which have touched the lives of thousands of people. Her extensive experience and dedication have helped attendees discover their passion, use their gifts and reach their full potential.

For more information all to work with Fernanda visit her website: fernandalorenti.com

Manal Akkad

Chapter Seven

Manal's early memories of growing up was: "Well this sucks, I'm going to do something about it." And so she did…

Born in Lebanon, during the Civil War, and raised into a fairly conservative environment. She grew up challenging social dogmas or what she refers to as cultural constipation which led her into doing things differently than what was expected from her, yet ordinary in her mind.

She left her hometown seeking opportunities, spent ten years in the Gulf, building her career working in Marketing and Advertising with multinational corporations, traveling the world thriving in her job, including but not limited to achieving double-digit growth for consecutive years. Manal was formally recognized through several personal and business awards.

After facing her biggest breakdown which challenged her to take a different course of action in life, she quit her high heels and pencil skirt and went on a mission of redefining her life.

Currently, she is living in Bali getting trained to serve as an embracing change mentor.

When you ask Manal what's her definition, she says, "I'm an ordinary woman, doing ordinary things to promote a world of ordinaries, just the way it should be."

Tasha Dietha Amanda

CHAPTER EIGHT

Born Tasha Dietha Amanda, is a native of Bontang Kaltim Indonesia. A self-educated entrepreneur, after graduating from school in Kalimantan, Tasha decided to pursue her career as a flight attendant in Jakarta. She joined PT. AirAsia Indonesia where she gained formal training. Her years as a flight attendant were tremendous. She was fervent, and so she was promoted twice before she decided to resign to start a business.

Tasha was hopeful, and she delved into the entrepreneurship world brilliantly. Her debut business was paper export, in which she used to discover her strengths and weaknesses as a new partner in the business. To enhance her knowledge and skills, she read a lot and spent a lot of time searching for information online to educate herself. Tasha faced so many obstacles while maintaining a thriving business.

Today, Tasha is the co-founder of a successful commodity business.

Pendek Sitong

CHAPTER NINE

Pendek Sitong was born in Bandung village, Boana, Lae, Morobe Province, Papua New Guinea. She is the first born child who was born in the absences of her father, Mr. Timbiong Sitong.

She was raised in another Province in Papua New Guinea and battled with poverty and psychological, verbal and physical abuse by an alcoholic dad. Pendek was forced to pick up bottles on the streets to make ends meet for the day, living one day at a time. It was during these trying times sleeping in caves that she made up her mind to study and get a job and change the way she lived.

After Pendek graduated at Divine Word University in 1990 with a diploma in College Of Allied Health Sciences, she gained employment as a Health Extension Officer. She has worked hard and sponsored many other people who were orphans, disabled and marginalized whenever she could. She has sponsored three orphans who have graduated with diplomas.

She is currently the District Health Manageress of Huon District Health Services and is in charge of 65 health workers. Taking care of the overall management and administration of Huon District Health Services in Morobe Province, Papua New Guinea the position she has occupied since 2004 until now.

Eui J Jung

CHAPTER TEN

Eui Jung Jung prefers to be called 'JJ,' because he has two Js in his name.

JJ was born in Incheon, Korea in one of the families of 'Internally Displaced People (IDP)' from the Korean War. For 20 years he was raised by his parents. For 25 years JJ served in the Republic of Korea Navy, including four years in the Naval Academy. He retired in 2016 and had a new lease on life.

During his journey, a question has been imprinted on his mind. And he is on his quest for an answer, which doesn't necessarily have to be right or wrong, or judgmental.

Life and Death, Vipassana meditation, Chen Taichi, and Toastmasters are his favorite topics. And Megalithic structure, Sanskrit civilization, and the Universe are also his favorite subjects. It all starts from within. Explore!

You can contact JJ at:

twojungs2@gmail.com

https://www.facebook.com/twojungs2

Afterword

I hope you enjoyed the collection of heartfelt stories, wisdom and vulnerability shared. Storytelling is the oldest form of communication, and I hope you feel inspired to take a step toward living a fulfilling life. Feel free to contact any of the authors in this book or the other books in this series.

The proceeds of this book will go to the Bali Street Kids Project, in Denpasar, Bali.

The project gives orphaned and abandoned children a home, meals and an education.

You can donate to this fantastic cause here: http://ykpa.org/

Other books in the series are…

Transformational Change: A Journey Of Riches, Book Twelve
https://www.amazon.com/dp/B07FYHMQRS

Finding Inspiration: A Journey Of Riches, Book Eleven
https://www.amazon.com/dp/B07F1LS1ZW

Building your Life from Rock Bottom: A Journey Of Riches, Book Ten
https://www.amazon.com/Building-your-Life-Rock-Bottom-ebook/dp/B07CZK155Z?pd_rd_wg=QoVt3&pd_rd_r=21874ec8-c199-43a0-9f7c-6b37a2c5cb86&pd_rd_w=BHfGz&ref

Transformation Calling: A Journey Of Riches, Book Nine
https://www.amazon.com/Transformation-Calling-Journey-John-Spender-ebook/dp/B07BWQY9FB/

Letting Go and Embracing the New: A Journey Of Riches, Book Eight
https://www.amazon.com/Letting-Go-Embracing-New-Journey/dp/0648284506/

Making Empowering Choices: A Journey Of Riches, Book Seven
https://www.amazon.com/Making-Empowering-Choices-Journey-Riches-ebook/dp/B078JXMK5V

The Benefit of Challenge: A Journey Of Riches, Book Six
https://www.amazon.com/Benefit-Challenge-Journey-Riches-ebook/dp/B0778S2VBD/

Personal Changes: A Journey Of Riches, Book Five
https://www.amazon.com/Personal-Changes-Journey-John-Spender-ebook/dp/B075WCQM4N/

Dealing with Changes in Life: A Journey Of Riches, Book Four
https://www.amazon.com/Dealing-Changes-Life-Motivational-Inspirational-ebook/dp/B0716RDKK7/

Making Changes: A Journey Of Riches, Book Three
https://www.amazon.com/Making-Changes-Journey-changes-Spiritual-ebook/dp/B01MYWNI5A/

The Gift In Challenge: A Journey Of Riches, Book Two
https://www.amazon.com/Gift-Challenge-Self-Help-Anthology-Spiritual-ebook/dp/B01GBEML4G/

From Darkness into the Light: A Journey Of Riches, Book One
https://www.amazon.com/Darkness-into-Light-Motivation-Inspiration-ebook/dp/B018QMPHJW/

Afterword

Thank you to all the authors that have shared aspects of their lives in the hope that it will inspire others to live a bigger version of themselves. I heard a great saying from Jim Rohan "You can't complain and feel grateful at the same time" at any given moment we have a chose to either feel like a victim of life or connected and grateful for it. I hope this book helps you to feel grateful go after your dreams.

www.ingramcontent.com/pod-product-compliance
Lightning Source LLC
Chambersburg PA
CBHW071929290426
44110CB00013B/1535